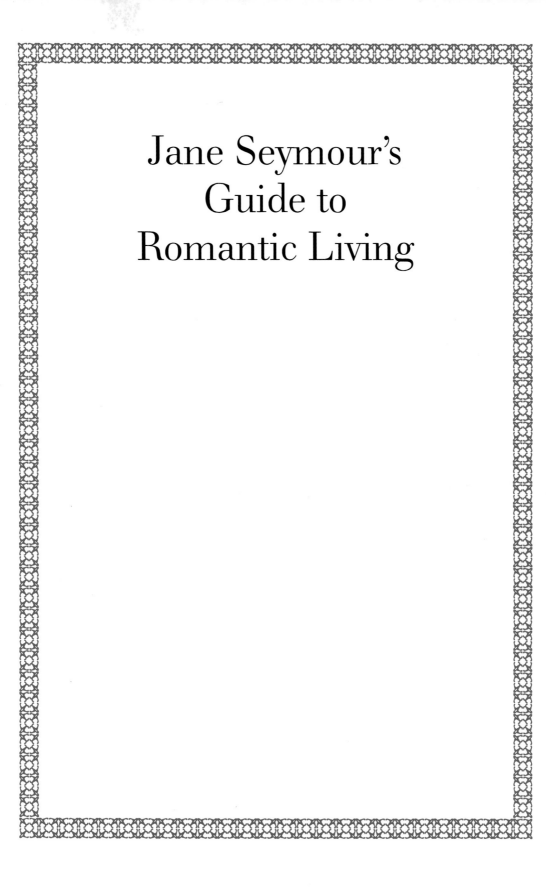

Jane Seymour's Guide to Romantic Living

JANE SEYMOUR'S
GUIDE TO
Romantic Living

⊞ ⊞ ⊞

JANE SEYMOUR

New York

ATHENEUM

1987

Seymour, Jane.
  Jane Seymour's Guide to romantic living.

1. Love. 2. Interpersonal relations. 3. Self-
actualization (Psychology) I. Title. II. Title: Guide
to romantic living.
HQ801.S46   1986   306.7   86-47675
ISBN 0-689-11786-8

Published simultaneously in Canada by Collier Macmillan Canada, Inc.
Composition by Graphic Composition, Athens, Georgia
Manufactured by Kingsport Press, Kingsport, Tennessee
Designed by Kathleen Carey
First Printing September 1986
Second Printing November 1986
Third Printing February 1987

To my husband, David,
who inspires me constantly,
and my parents,
who introduced me to Romantic Living.

Acknowledgements

There are so many people I'd like to thank for helping me with this book. Without these people's help I could never have fulfilled this romantic fantasy—the book.

My family—David, Katie, Sean, Jenni, Mummy and P, Sally and Anne; David's parents, Olga and Lloyd.

And—Brian Aris, Laura Ashley, Laurie Bernstein, Martin Bernstein, Steven Bickel, Daracie Bond, Skip Brittenham, Butler and Wilson, Cartier, Yanou Collart, Sally Emerson, David and Elizabeth Emmanuel, Susan Ginsburg, Larry Dale Gordon, Stacey Hallett, Joy Harris, Verna Harvey, Ellen Johnson, Jeff Jones, Layla and Essam Khashoggi, Peter Kredenser, Beverly Lee, David Leonard, Jane Lewis, Corinna Liddell, Bianca Nehring, Leslie Oliver, Steve Riley, Ann Garman Rittenberg, Esther Rosenfield, Johnny Rozsa, Heidi Schaeffer, Steve Schapiro, MB and Geonine Scott, Judy Tarlo, Clifford Haydon-Tovey, Dick Zimmerman.

Foreword

ONE day standing in the shower, newly pregnant
with my second baby and just finished with my latest
film, I wondered, Now what? I felt very content and
excited about the coming months but also felt I had
something I wanted to do or say during this time that
would express why, despite the normal dissatisfactions
with everyday life, I am basically happy.

I've never been a writer—indeed, it's the last talent
I could ever claim for myself—but I wanted to share
the passion I feel for life that makes it that much more
special. I know and have always known that I am a
very privileged person, not because of wealth or fame
or power or the usual things that one thinks of as be-
longing to privilege, but because I have a deep sense

of optimism, a sense of daring, an ability to make life better or more special, a belief that one can fulfill one's dreams, large or small. I have always taken the risk, never given up; even when everything appeared to be catastrophic, I felt it was possible to turn one's dream, one's fantasies, into reality. I have been poor at times and privileged at others, but always, when I watched people around me, people of all nationalities and walks of life, I realized that we all share life itself, and that it is the fulfillment of the romantic dream or the creation of a special moment that one never forgets, not the material rewards.

I think that romance is the creation of that special moment, that a romantic life is full of those creations. I want to share with you my beliefs about romance and its importance in every part of life, and I hope that by doing this I'll be able to impart the sense that, while it's important to lead a romantic life, it's also remarkably easy. It takes a heightened awareness of the world around you, being open to the romantic possibilities of a dinner at home, a business lunch, a vacation with your family, a rainy Sunday with your children. I'll show you how simple it is to transform your bedroom into a romantic haven, to bring a sense of romantic adventure to a children's birthday party, to create a romantic picnic from a local farmers' market, even to set the stage for a dramatically exciting dinner party. It doesn't require you to buy anything or to inherit a fortune, but it does require that you learn to know yourself and what you want out of life day to day. Whether you're a working mother who wants more time with her children or more time alone with her husband, a woman who thrives in an all-consuming career, a woman who stays home to care for her family's needs, or a single woman who supports herself, you can bring romance into your life. And you'll find that in sharing your desire for more of those special moments you'll enhance not only your own life but also the lives of the people around you.

This is not about the lifelong partner or the marriage of convenience or the one-night stand. It's about approaching your life with the drama and mystery that some of us think exists only in books, TV, and movies. Even though I make those movies, I find myself wishing that more of those magic moments could happen in real life. This book is about making it all come true.

I was born to two wonderful, unconventional, loving, and romantic parents. They gave their children all the opportunities they had missed: a life with education, no war, love, stability, and a great sense of security in being our own persons. We weren't rich at all, but never felt poor or lacking in any way. The special things we had and did came from our parents' sense of adventure and surprise, and this really is where my ideas spring from. Against the odds of their generation, the war, their age, their time in life, they have dared to live the romantic life. They've never been afraid to make romantic gestures, never been too busy to make the small gesture that means so much to those around them. They have shared their unique approach to life with many of my friends and theirs, and people always remember them for this. They enrich others' lives when they try to enrich their own.

Yes, I am a romantic. It's not the most practical thing to be, or the most profound thing to say, I agree, but when all is over, the sense of having lived, of having loved a lot, of having spent the precious time allotted to us on this planet positively and pleasurably with people who share these feelings, will make all the hassle worth it.

Women and men are uncertain now of their places in the world. One year women find freedom and in their understandable excitement at enjoying it fully leave men feeling left out and confused. The next year women find power and in their zeal at wielding what has so long been denied them they somehow overlook their birthright of an emotional, instinctive, sensual reaction to life.

Women, if they wish to, should allow themselves their femininity, their sense of motherhood, and their drive to accomplish. And men should continue to enjoy the chase, the image of the knight in shining armor. We should all celebrate our differences.

Little things are what affect everyone so much. The flower left casually by the bed, or on the desk, the gift for no apparent reason, the holiday (if only for two nights) that is a surprise, the note that was never expected. These little things make life richer and more special. Envying others for their success or money, possessions or power, doesn't enrich your life. Richness comes from living romantically—being surprising and mysterious, finding your own style and sharing it with your loved one, your friends, your children.

It is these things that I wanted to share while I awaited my second child, feeling the great privilege of happiness in a frantic and competitive world.

CONTENTS

CREDITS

Pages 49, 57 (bottom) 165: photographs by Brian Aris. Page 120 (bottom): photograph by Peter C. Borsari. Page 210: photograph by Steven Bickel. Page 124 (top): photograph by Charles Bush. Pages 37 (bottom), 129: photographs by Michel Comte. Page 91 (bottom): photograph by Zoe Dominic. Pages 193 (top), 193 (bottom), 203 (top): photographs by Larry Dale Gordon. Page 69: photograph by Steve Horn, courtesy of Max Factor. Pages 11 (top), 11 (bottom), 24 (top), 55, 65 (top left), 65 (bottom right), 102, 104 (bottom), 109 (bottom), 148, 156 (bottom), 160 (bottom), 170 (bottom), 172 (bottom), 175 (bottom), 175 (top), 179 (top), 179 (bottom), 181 (top), 181 (bottom), 184 (top), 184 (bottom), 191 (bottom), 200 (top), 207 (top): photographs by Peter Kredenser. Page 44: photograph by Doug McKenzie—P.P.S. Page 64 (bottom right): photograph by R. Melloul-Sygma. Page 163: photograph by Richard Nobel, courtesy of Max Factor. Page 9 (top): photograph by "P." Pages 39, 41, 95 (top), 96 (top), 97, 145 (bottom), 170 (top): photographs by Johnny Rozsa. Page 138 (top): photograph by Eddie Sanderson. Pages 20, 94, 109 (top), 152 (top), 152 (bottom), 154, 156 (top), cover, frontispiece: photographs by Steve Schapiro. Page 37 (top): photograph by Peter Stachiw. Page 124 (bottom): photograph by Jean Wadley. Page 127 (top): photograph by Julian Wasser. Pages 5, 24 (bottom), 33, 95 (bottom), 96 (bottom), 134 (top), 160 (top): photographs by Dick Zimmerman. Page 65 (top right): courtesy of C.B.S. Pages 64 (bottom left), 145 (top): courtesy of N.B.C. Photographic Department. Pages 6, 91 (top): © 1980 Universal Pictures. A Division of Universal City Studios, Inc. Courtesy of M.C.A. Publishing Rights, A Division of M.C.A. Inc. Page 65 (bottom left): courtesy of Paramount Pictures Corporation. © 1969 Paramount Pictures Corporation. All rights reserved. Pages 64 (top), 118: © 1984. A.C.&D. (Plant Hirers) Limited; PKC Finance: Henderson-Kenton Furnishing Limited, Minster House Limited. All rights reserved.

Hair and Make-up Page 5: hair by Elaine Freed. Pages 33, 95: hair and make-up by Jeff Jones. Page 5: make-up by Bobbe Joy. Pages 20, 37 (bottom), 69, 102, 107 (top), 109 (bottom), 124 (top), 129, 148, 163, 207 (top): hair and make-up by David Leonard—Thom Tamblyn, Inc. Page 129: make-up by Bonnie Maller. Pages 24 (bottom), 39, 41, 94, 95, 96, 97, 145 (bottom), 154, 160 (top), frontispiece: hair and make-up by Steven Reiley— H.M.S. Bookings. Pages 37 (bottom), 129: hair by John Sahag—John Sahag Salon, N.Y. Page 24 (top): hair and make-up by Jetty Stutzman—Cloutier.

Gowns Pages Frontispiece, 41, 97: Emanuel. Page 102: Grace Costumes/Geoffrey Holder. Page 57: Laura Ashley (girls), Lezlie Oliver (Jane). Page 65 (bottom right): Nolan Miller. Page 94: Diamond et Noir. Page 24 (bottom): Martin Bernstein.

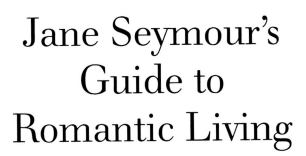

Jane Seymour's Guide to Romantic Living

1

The Romantic Attitude

I HOPE this is a book that will change your life. I'm going to tell you how to live life romantically, how to get the most out of every moment. I want you to realize, as I did, that you can be the person you wish to be. I want you to see your dream person and to become that person. Your dream person needn't remain a figment of your imagination. You can walk right into your dreams and come out a new person.

Of course, it's risky. Any kind of change is risky. But if you're going to get the most out of your life you must grasp its pleasures along the way. You must be receptive.

I realize, now that I have children of my own, that I

was taught all this in childhood. Above the mantelpiece in my parents' house in England there is still a picture of me and my two sisters: three girls dressed as ballerinas, wearing blue headbands, with our hair piled up into buns. Our faces are graceful, our necks long, our posture perfect. At the time of the portrait we were in fact just three quite pretty girls of six, seven, and eight with normal plumpness. But the idealized portrait caught hold of my imagination. I wanted to be that person.

All my life I have done this—seen an image in my mind and tried to create it, to bring it alive. Perhaps the image in your mind is of you and a hazily pictured lover walking on the beach. He stoops to kiss you as the waves crash in. My point is: make it happen. But don't make it happen with a dream lover—turn your husband, your long-term boyfriend, or the man you've just started dating into that lover. Make a dream out of everyday reality, then make reality out of a dream. That's what my parents taught me to do.

My mother had plenty of time to dream. She spent the war in a Japanese prisoner-of-war camp in Indonesia (where she lived at the time). There was never enough to eat. To get through those difficult years she used to imagine a big family house that was always warm and full of food, people, and happiness. After the war, when she met my father and married him, she achieved her dream with startling rapidity. In three years they had three children and in another few years we were settled in a rambling Victorian house with a huge lawn (to my child's eye it seemed huge), a vegetable garden, a beehive, a swing, and endless bedrooms.

Nothing makes you feel more romantic than beautiful lingerie—even when you wear it under a business suit.

My parents weren't rich, but they weren't poor, and everything they had was spent on living: breakfasts that went on and on all morning as guests from home or abroad came down to eat; Indonesian feasts for lunch which seldom started before three or four; dinners for unknown numbers at a moment's notice—doctors, architects, people speaking different languages, people of all ages. This was life on a grand scale, but I assumed it was normal until I visited other people's more conventional homes. It wasn't extravagant; it was simply exuberant. Our life was my mother's dream come true.

My mother ran the household eccentrically and brilliantly while also running a business selling everything under the sun to foreign embassies in London. She even sold caviar and vodka to the Russian embassy. I think the embassies were under the impression they were dealing with a huge firm, not one determined woman shutting herself up in an office in between one household event and another. But my father was very much the head of the household. (My mother was certainly old-fashioned in that respect.) We were taught to admire him and to respect him. When he demanded quiet, we gave him quiet. Otherwise my mother's dream of a full family life could have clashed nastily with my father's more scholarly nature.

It was his dreams for me that were the inspiration for my career and that still inspire me. He helped to make every day of our lives a romantic adventure. I can see him now, sitting in his armchair with his glasses on, putting the finishing touches to the Christmas pantomime he had written for us three girls and our friends. (He is one of England's foremost gynecologists but sometimes I think he'd have loved to have been a writer most of all.) He didn't just write the pantomime, he filmed it with a movie camera. It is something any father could have done, but how many actually make the effort? We still have the film, a little crackly; I play Cinderella. He introduced us to classical music by encouraging us to create ballets which we performed out on the lawn. One minute I was little Joyce Frankenberg from Wimbledon (I later changed it to Jane Seymour), the next my sisters and I and our friends were dancing wildly over the lawn to the music of Vivaldi's *The Four Seasons.* What could be more romantic? My parents turned the house and garden into the Royal Ballet one day, a film studio the next.

My father created dreams for us everywhere, and they all caught my imagination, but the one that caught it most of all was that of becoming a ballerina. At the age of thirteen I went to a professional ballet school, and if it hadn't been for a knee injury I would still, I think, be an average ballerina today. Instead, I followed my next-best fantasy: to become an actress.

I still share my career with my parents—and am always asking their advice. Before I had my children, I played Bathsheba in the television film *King David.* The part required me to give birth on screen, the first time I'd ever been asked to do so. I called my father up and said, "Tell me how to be pregnant and how to give birth—where the pains come from, what they are like."

In the film, some Spanish gypsies were extras around me. There was no rehearsal; the cameras were just turned on and I went into "labor." My father's advice was so good that the gypsy women thought it was for real and went running around looking for water.

The crew had to explain to the women that I was only acting.

* * *

In many ways I seem to live a life out of a romantic novel: handsome husband, two lovely children, marvelous Los Angeles house, magical stately home in England, a good career as an actress. But of course the reality is much of the time anyone's reality, the problems ordinary problems. Sometimes I'm so caught up in planning and juggling and worrying that I lose all sense of how lucky I am. And this is the point: romance doesn't come automatically to someone with long hair or a stately home. Romance is an attitude, a state of mind. Like all the best qualities, it comes from within; you just have to look for it and know how to develop it. It is this that I am going to share with you in the pages of this book. You can't sit back and accept life. You've got to seize it, as my parents taught me, whether it's waking up early one morning and going out for a walk at dawn or making your partner an unexpected breakfast in bed complete with champagne. It's wearing silky underwear beneath an executive suit. It's swimming naked at night in a warm pool. It's realizing that life is there to be altered, to be made more interesting, to be lived the way you want and dare to live it.

Life is not a fairy tale—even my life is not a fairy tale—but at times, if I try hard enough, I believe I can turn it into one. In England, I often ride my horse in the early morning with my husband, David, and it's the dew, the air, the sounds of the birds, all the

Mummy's favorite pastime: looking at photographs—memories of good times.

*My Dutch grandmother
at the turn of the century.*

The famous photograph from Somewhere in Time
later reminded me of Granny.

things that are available and free to anyone, that are romantic.

It's making each day fresh—noticing things. At our house in England I send my daughter, Katie, out searching for leaves and flowers which we look at and label together. It helps make her appreciate the wonder and excitement of everything around her.

The world is a miraculous place, full of marvelous things. But you have to be able to see them. You have to look. Being alive is romantic so long as you don't get so weighed down by your work and responsibilities that you can no longer see how lucky you really are, how wonderful life can be. You have to try to be happy, of course. It doesn't happen by magic. I fail often—I work too hard, I get weighed down by things, I lose my temper, my enthusiasm. But there's always tomorrow.

My life isn't exactly a textbook description of an old-fashioned life of fidelity and romance. I'm on my third marriage. I had had two divorces by the time I was thirty. Not very good going. But I've learned. I've been through it, and I've learned my lessons. And now I know what's important for me.

The marriages and divorces have not been easy. I married two very romantic men of whom I still am very fond, although I know now that we never would have achieved long-term marriages.

In those days I was obsessed with my career. I would give up anyone and anything to go off and do another movie. That was my childishness. It took me until my thirties to realize what it was that I really wanted and how important that was and how I could use my romantic nature to build on what I had rather than searching for what I hadn't. During my life I have

A wild goose chase.

Katie and I collecting leaves.

thrown myself into quite a few relationships that maybe I should have thought about more seriously beforehand. I was the ultimate romantic. Each one had to be special and extraordinary. But what I've learned now, and one reason why this book is so important to me, is that there is a way for all of us to live romantically without living foolishly, a way of combining hard work with romance.

Few people nowadays have much leisure time to devote to the beauty of life and to thinking about romance and how to keep their marriages or love affairs exciting. And look at the results: broken families, broken hearts, broken lives. We concentrate on our careers, on running a home efficiently, on governing the country, and we look around and discover the thing we needed most of all—a happy and stable partnership—has gone.

Romance is vital. We must bring it back into this century of office blocks and superwomen. Romance matters to every woman, to the young girl who is not married, to the hard-working woman with a career and no children, and to the woman who has a marriage, career, and children. Nowadays we all have to juggle continually. There is never any time. But all the juggling will be pointless, a parade of a useless skill, if while parading that skill we forget to live. The precious moments, the grace and style and delight and tenderness, are all there, waiting to be found. But if you take things too seriously you'll never find them, and you'll regret the flowers you didn't buy, the walks you didn't take, the picnics you didn't plan.

The older woman, too, the woman whose children have left home and for whom some of the juggling has stopped, needs romance, perhaps to fill some of the stillness left behind when the action has stopped. Look at my mother, for instance. She's over seventy, like my father, yet they live the life of romantic teenagers. They travel all over the world, constantly. They're not wealthy; they stay with the friends they have made, and when they're at home in England their friends stay with them. One of my sisters, Sally, works for an airline, so she provides them with cheap airline tickets. They have a marvelous time. It's because of their romantic attitude toward life that they make so many close friends: they are fun to be with, they're not rigid, they will go along with any plan, any scheme, they take each day as it comes. They're very happy together. Recently, in Portugal, my mother heard the birds singing at five in the morning. Instead of groaning, she woke my father up, and together they went down to the beach and sat hand in hand watching the sunrise. This is romance.

Let us not treat life as an obstacle race, with a frown on our faces, something to get through. Instead, let's enjoy it, and give our children the background to enjoy it. Let us not lose that most romantic of things: freedom. I don't mean we must all be vagabonds. It's the freedom of spirit that matters, and it is that that helps make a romantic partnership.

We live in a material age. We are always trying to improve our lot but too often this means changing the circumstances of our lives. When the vacuum cleaner doesn't work we get a new one. When our car isn't as smart as someone else's we change it. But when we take this attitude into our personal lives it's not so simple. If we're not completely happy with our husband, we decide our relationship with him is obsolete. We don't bother to mend old cars, so we don't see that our relationship needs mending, needs freshness, needs romance. The answer is not to find a new lover, it is to turn your husband into the lover. The answer for a young unmarried girl is not to sit alone reading romantic novels, it is to go out and find your romantic hero, to turn that shy chap at the far end of the room into the man for you.

It's *you* who has to change, who has to make things happen for you. The pattern of the leaves is there for anyone. Of course it's romantic going to Paris, but it's also romantic to walk along any beach at midnight, hand in hand. More romantic, actually, because it's not prepackaged romance. There's not that awful business of thinking, oh, this is expensive, we must enjoy it. Real romance is free, but it requires thought and love and a certain tenderness, and more than a little imagination.

It is hard to be open to change while under constant pressure. Women's liberation has freed us from many of our chains and provided us with a whole new set of them: now we have to be perfect mothers, perfect wives, brilliant careerwomen. There does not appear to be time anymore to be happy. It is hard to fit it into the schedule. One friend of mine, who lives in New York, takes a "mental health day" every so often, during which she leaves her three children with the baby sitter and goes off with her husband as if going to work, but instead of going to work they simply wander around. Nothing is planned. They have breakfast in some cheap breakfast place, they wander about the streets, they become as they used to be before the work ethic took its toll and drove them both into frantic, planned-to-the-minute office and home life.

Work is important. We certainly don't want to lose what women have struggled for so many years to achieve. In fact, I should declare right now that I am one of the most ambitious and dedicated people I have come across. But I still know that it is David, my children, my family, and my home that matter to me most, and if I were ever to lose them I would lose everything. That's one reason I wanted to write this book, to remind people not to lose all the old values, not to change roles overnight. Women need men. And men need women.

I think a lot of people are beginning to realize that they were in danger of forgetting this, and that's why romance is back.

CHILDHOOD

Meeting sister Sally — she newly born, me 15 months

With my father

Me, newborn, with mummy

School production, age fifteen

"acting" in school uniform

Feeding the ducks and
daydreaming, age 3

First dancing costume, age 3

Three sisters as ballerinas

The three sisters in one of
our family plays

2

Finding Your Romantic Self

Too many people treat life as though it's the dress rehearsal for some big show. It's not. This is it. You're onstage now. Stop *preparing* to live—start *living*.

Over the course of this book I'll probably endlessly refer to my husband and to how wonderful he is, because he is. He has brought out the romantic in me more than any man I've ever known. But that doesn't mean that you need a man to be your most romantic self. You can be romantic on your own—by reacting to life in a way that is both vulnerable and individualistic. It is romantic to dress in your own way, to behave in your own way, to become yourself, not somebody else's idea of what you should be, not what someone told you to be. It is romantic to want to live in beautiful surroundings, to watch the birds, to keep your mystery. Whether or not you share all this with a husband or lover is hardly relevant to whether you are romantic or not.

I want to take you toward an understanding that anyone or anything can be romantic. I am saying that all of this is marvelous, all of it: being single, or being alone, or having a lover, or having plenty of lovers, or having a husband. I am not just talking to those who feel their marriages are dull—I'm talking to those who feel their lives are dull, that some of the ardor has gone out of living. I'm talking to women who have never read a romantic novel, and to those who read them constantly to escape the drabness all around. I'm not much of a reader, and I don't like watching television all that often (what a confession from someone dubbed "The Queen of the Mini Series"). I like to turn life into drama. I like to be the heroine of my own life—to be vulnerable, soft, mysterious, and yet strong and individualistic too. I like to be different people on different days, to keep everyone guessing.

We are all too used to being passive. We accept too much. We look to movies and television for the excitement and drama in our lives. Take your life in hand and be your own heroine. Become Scarlett O'Hara (a successful businesswoman too, remember?), be the mysterious heroine of contemporary romantic novels. Don't stride around in identical business clothes, like all the other women: be yourself. Don't try to be a man. Don't accept—create.

Your image of yourself can encompass many different people. I can be a wild sexy creature but I'm also the Victorian lady who can sit and do needlepoint for

19

My first attempt at real Hollywood glamour!!

hours on end, covered in lace, with my feet on a little cushion. I can also be the eighties woman who loves to work out in a gym and lift weights and sweat and feel the muscles burn. I am a lot of different women in one—I think everyone is. Use your imagination. Be the person you want to be, be all the different women you think you are, make life what you want it to be.

Even the most unexciting of things—food in a hospital ward—can be transformed with a little imagination. The night after I had my first baby, my husband, David, came to the hospital with a big cardboard box. In the box were the plates, the cutlery, the napkins, and an entire meal from my favorite restaurant, along with a bottle of champagne. Of course the chocolate nut sundae had melted, but that wasn't important. Even the quality of the food wasn't important. It was the imagination that mattered. Any man could carefully prepare a beautiful picnic to bring to his wife in the hospital. Champagne isn't necessary, expense isn't necessary; it's the imagination and tenderness that are moving.

As I've said before, and will say many times—because to me it's one of the most important things in the world—romance is an attitude of mind. It's treating ordinary life and convention as merely the raw material for your own life. You don't have to bring someone flowers or fruit in the hospital, like everyone else does. Take a minute's thought. Think freshly. Don't be weighed down by what has been done, by what is usually done. On the other hand, just because no one dresses for dinner or the theater or sends thank-you notes after a party anymore doesn't mean you can't. Make your own romantic gestures. The husband of a friend of mine was coming to pick her up for a quick dinner one Friday after work. She thought he sounded tired, so to surprise him she made a reservation at one of their favorite small restaurants and asked that a bottle of champagne be chilled and waiting for them. Not only was he surprised and delighted at the gesture, but everyone at the restaurant—waiter, bartender, owners—had enormous fun being in on the secret. It isn't hard to take trouble and thought over things. It's easier to be a robot, trundling efficiently through the days. You can get through life that way without too much bother, but who wants to live like that? You're bound to feel discontented. Make life your own. Don't just accept other people's versions of it. Turn it into an adventure, and make your life, and the lives of those you love, marvelous in the process.

David is a great actor. He's never acted professionally in his life but he has a flair for drama, for turning the ordinary into the extraordinary. One time we took a trip to New York that was supposed to be a magical holiday for us both, but in fact we both worked and hardly saw each other at all. The night we were at the "Night of 100 Stars," a big charity show, we rushed around like lunatics and I had only half an hour's break. On top of everything, it was my birthday and he hadn't given me anything, not even a card. We eventually ended up in a restaurant, where David ordered some champagne. But all I really wanted at that moment was some water.

"Could I have some Perrier, please?" I said to the waiter.

The waiter brought me Perrier in a champagne glass. I couldn't understand why he brought me Perrier in a champagne glass, and why there was so little. I felt like saying: "That's not much Perrier. I'd like a whole glass, please." Then I looked down into the glass and saw something glinting at the bottom, just covered with the bubbly, sparkling Perrier.

It was a beautiful ring.

Of course, David had been in cahoots with the head-waiter and had arranged the whole event ahead of time. His moodiness and forgetfulness had been a show. He had made me wait and then, when I least expected it, had surprised me.

The point of this story is that romance often comes from the unexpected. And the unexpected can be planned, but it requires a little showmanship.

I know someone who didn't have any money, so he bought his girlfriend an engagement ring from a bubble-gum machine and presented it to her in a glass of champagne. Who could resist a man who did that? It shows nerve, vitality, mischief, and the most terrific sense of romance.

She accepted him at once.

It's this sort of stage management that is so impressive and turns life into a fantasy, with you and your lover playing the star roles. Why not? Why settle for second best? Why not turn your life into a fantasy of your own creation? Why not direct it, star in it, and produce it? Enjoy yourself. Have fun.

As Andrew Marvell wrote in his great love poem "To His Coy Mistress": "The grave's a fine and private place,/But none, I think, do there embrace."

The showmanship doesn't have to lead to a grand event, to a diamond ring, to a marriage proposal, to a seduction; it can just be a way of making little things

LEFT: *A single rose can be so special.*

Feathers and tapestry—an exotic look.

special. For instance, if a woman arranges lunch and dinner for her husband and family in the dining room every day, and then one day puts the table outside, under the oak tree, that is romantic because it breaks away from the usual, the everyday. Or if a man one night puts a flower on his wife's pillow, or gets up before her one morning and makes coffee and brings it to her in bed, that's romantic. One boyfriend used to leave notes for me everywhere before he went away— hidden in all kinds of unexpected places so that I'd come across them gradually. One would say, "You are beautiful," another, "How are you today?," another "I love you." I found them in the sugar, behind the kettle, everywhere, and it kept me close to him while he was away.

For one of my friends romance is the day her husband hired the London Philharmonic to play outside her window on her birthday, for another it's the day her lover brought her a bunch of violets when she was ill. The point is that it's something that makes life different, that shows care and tenderness and a sense that each day is not laid out on a plate. Anything can happen. We make the days, and we can make them good for ourselves and for others.

What everyone should remember is that you can do anything, try any role. There are no rules. The only way you can discover how best to live your life is to try out new ideas. Every week David and I have a business lunch at which we discuss everything to do with money, so that we don't have to clutter the rest of our lives with it. It sounds odd, I suppose. But David used to accuse me of hitting him with a problem just as he was walking out the door, so we decided that instead of talking about business problems at home, we would talk about them where he ordinarily goes for his male business lunches. I'm usually the only woman there. And people keep looking at us and wondering how we could possibly be having such a nice time together while presumably discussing business. (It's not at all the sort of place you would choose if you were planning a romantic tryst.) But our lunches are romantic because they are out of the ordinary, and they allow us to have time to be more romantic at home. It's almost like having a date.

Part of what I'll be talking about throughout this book is the importance of being open to change, of allowing yourself to be receptive, of playing different roles at different times—to be the efficient business-lunch date with your husband or lover, to surprise him, to manage your life with imagination. Life isn't a pre-packaged factory-made product: you make it yourself.

As an actress I'm used to playing different roles and of course I enjoy it. And that is one of the things I want to pass on to other people: the pleasures of being creative with your life, of stepping out of your usual routines and becoming someone or something else, even if only for a short time. Anything can be changed, even your name. A new name can make all the difference in the world to your life. It did to mine.

I took the name Jane Seymour because nobody considered my real name, Joyce Frankenberg (Joyce Penelope Wilhemena Frankenberg, to be precise), balletic enough. They said, not without accuracy, that it could be confused with Frankenstein, frankfurter, and frankenburger. First, I used a number of different names, to try them out. I registered half a dozen with

The Marquis of Hertford, a direct descendant of the original Jane Seymour, posing with his Holbein portrait of her at his home, Ragley Hall, where I was filming The Scarlet Pimpernel.

Actors' Equity. The one that lasted longest was Joya Johns, which was based on the Italian word for joy, *gioia*, and my father's name, John. It meant John's joy.

I didn't change my name to Jane Seymour, the name of Henry VIII's third wife, until I was with my first agent, at the age of seventeen.

It was my agent's nephew who came up with the name. Everyone said, "Gosh, that name is familiar." But surprisingly, not many knew why. Perhaps because at that time all those movies about Henry VIII and his six wives hadn't been made.

I took the name and instantly started having meetings with people on projects. It turned my career around, because people would say to my agent, "I'm sure I've met her somewhere." And my agent would never say, "You've heard of her because she was the wife of Henry the Eighth, idiot." He just said, "Yes, she really is terrific and I'm glad you want to meet her."

At one time, well on in my career, in Hollywood, I was asked to meet Dino di Laurentiis. He sat me down in his office and told me how wonderful I'd been in his film *Anne of the Thousand Days*, about Henry VIII and Anne Boleyn. I tried to interrupt and tell him I hadn't been in the film, but he raved on and on.

Eventually, I simply and quietly mustered a gracious "Thank you."

Change your name, change the color of your hair, change your habits, experiment in order to discover who you are. Don't just think, I am this person who has dark hair and is called such and such and lives at such and such an address. Your real self, who is perhaps waiting for you to discover her, might have blond hair or bright red hair, she might wear glasses or own a pair of frivolous shoes or go out on blind dates. Try something different.

Have you ever wondered if, deep inside you, you really wanted to be a redhead, have a curly mop, or be a blonde? I took my publisher out the other day to relax while putting this book together. We thought of buying a pair of shoes or something for the kids, but as luck would have it, we came to a wig store and laughed at all the crazy things in the window. I suggested that we go in. I tried on several wigs, knowing how useful it might be for my career to have different options in the hair department, and then I suggested she try them too. Like many people, she claimed to be at her wit's end trying to find a good hair style and cut, so she tried on a wig in her own color. Suddenly, it was a whole new her. I bought it for her and one for me, and when she met her husband later, he thought she looked great. It lifted her day and mine—she now knows what to aim for with her hair—and has a fun new look while she waits.

Dressing, loving, cooking—everything can be different, enhanced, if you only experiment. Even something as mundane as bathing can be transformed into an exquisite experience. One friend likes to give her husband a facial and a massage in the bath. He loves it. He says: "Wives don't do this. Only girlfriends or mistresses do this." She fills the bath and turns the lights down very low. Then she lights a scented candle—smells are important to romance—and puts on some soft music, Mozart or Vivaldi—something very sensual. Then they both climb into the bath. She puts a little oil in the water, lines up some creams and oils, and gives him a facial. He lies in the bath with his head on her chest and she works her hands over his face.

But you can be romantic when you're alone. There's nothing quite as heavenly as a big old-fashioned bubble bath, in which you can lounge and dream for an hour or more, topping it up with hot water, while listening to your favorite romantic music by candle-light.

If you think positively and romantically, the miracle is that people will be attracted to you and the presence around you. They will want to be near you. If you think negatively and drearily, people will stay away in droves. Make an event out of everything you do. Remember life isn't something you just have to get through: it's here for you to enjoy.

3

Bringing Romance to Everyday Life

THE dictionary tells us that a romance is a tale with scenes and incidents remote from everyday life. But romance needn't be remote. It can be part of everyday life.

It is easy to become so weighed down by work and worry that you cease to notice the marvels all around you. Some years ago I was playing Ophelia up in the North of England and staying in awful digs miles away from any family or friends. I was very depressed, very hemmed in by the bad weather and gloomy city. Then someone suggested that a group of us go for a drive. We piled into a car, and it wasn't long before we found ourselves on the most beautiful moors, covered with mist, like a scene from *Macbeth*. We were ten feet apart and yet we couldn't see each other. We kept appearing and disappearing through the mist. The atmosphere was very strange, very romantic, very beautiful. And those moors, the Yorkshire Moors, had been there all the time, just a short distance away from the town we were complaining about so much.

That is the point: the extraordinary is always there, waiting just around a corner, only a car ride away—all you have to do is break the pattern of depression or gloom or stifling ordinariness to find it. If you're fed up, look at a map and find the nearest green space. It might be the site of a ruined castle. It might be covered in bluebells. You might arrive there just as a storm breaks out and you can sit in the car as the rain batters against the windows and reminds you how close you are all the time to the rain, and the lightning, and the sea, and all the things that make life splendid. Anything might happen.

Don't be someone so busy achieving, overreaching, that you never really notice anything. Live in the present, not in the future. Don't lose your imagination, your capacity to live and enjoy the present. Above all, don't be afraid to do something different.

Your imagination and invention can be the fairy godmother that transforms you from Cinderella into the beautiful woman who stuns everyone at the ball. It really can. You can be anyone, do anything. Anything can happen, from now on.

The passive, dreamily "romantic" girl of the past is finished with. We don't want to return to that. We don't want to be dim, pretty, passive creatures, however much some men might think they like that. I am arguing for women becoming actively, positively, imagi-

With Katie in our favorite dresses.

natively romantic: combining the genuine advances of feminism with our most precious qualities: femininity, intuition, imagination.

If you feel you would like to wear a velvet gown but don't dare: dare. If you can't afford one: make it yourself. Learn to sew, and sew beautifully. Nothing is impossible if you want it enough. When I was out of work as an actress in England, I used to embroider blouses for me, my friends, and to sell in top London shops. The embroidery looked difficult but with concentration and patience it wasn't at all. Never be put off because something looks difficult. If you concentrate properly you can do anything. If you allow yourself to be distracted—to flit from subject to subject—you'll do nothing well.

Feminism tells us to take charge of our own destinies. There is nothing wrong with that. But I'm arguing for something slightly different: don't take charge of your destiny merely to compete with men. In doing so you admittedly gain a great deal—status, money, respect—but you are liable to lose a great deal too. You can lose your femininity. You can turn men into frightened weaklings, emasculated creatures with whom you wouldn't want to have an affair even if they summoned up the courage to ask you. Have the sense to hold onto your femininity.

You can be the heroine of your own life. Use your determination, your courage, your self-respect, all those things that feminism has helped to give us, to become a romantic heroine. Heroines are all around us: Jane Fonda is one of mine. But there are so many others, from the past as well as the present: there's Cleopatra, Catherine the Great, Florence Nightingale,

Mary Shelley, Gertrude Bell and other women travelers, writers Colette, Jane Austen, the Brontës. Examine their lives. What is it about each one that you admire so much? Why shouldn't you be like that? What is stopping you? It isn't enough merely to dream—add just something of their splendor to your own, more ordinary, life.

Take the great French writer Colette, for instance. Of all her love affairs, the deepest and most passionate was with nature. In childhood her mother had showed her how to look and to wonder. When Colette was close to death, lying in her Paris flat, crippled with arthritis, "Look—look," she said and tried to raise her arm to point at the bird on her window sill, her eyes as fresh with excitement and wonder as when she was a child. Of all her achievements and dramas, that is what I respect most. She kept her freshness. And that is something anyone can do if they try. You can learn to look. Even if you are not a good artist it is worth putting aside a little time every now and again to try to draw a tree, or a person, or a bird, or a flower. By trying to draw you can learn to see. You can observe what is extraordinary about an ordinary bird, as Colette did. Someone who observes the world, who is close to the world, will be close to her own self, too.

We are all so used to being in control of our worlds that sometimes it is hard to cease to control. It is hard simply to see, to feel, to listen, to be passive instead of active. It is hard for the careerwoman who comes home from work to take immediate notice of her children, to listen to them, watch them, to make the transition from the active work person to the passive, watchful, patient mother. But making that transition smoothly has its own rewards, as I have discovered on more than one occasion.

Recently I returned from filming some of my part as Natalie Jastrow in the television film of Herman Wouk's epic *War and Remembrance.* I had the flu. I was physically exhausted from traveling around Europe and emotionally exhausted from helping to reenact the Holocaust (I am half Jewish, on my father's side). I had lost ten pounds and was supposed to be back home on holiday for a week, but the moment I arrived I was told that filming would resume in two days and that I'd have to fly back then.

When I got home what I needed more than anything else was love and attention, and I demanded it. But Katie wanted the nanny, not me, and wouldn't even come into my bed in the morning, which she normally loves to do. My husband had organized his life as a bachelor and was busy with his polo and his horses, and my baby didn't recognize me. I simply didn't belong in that house. I was a stranger. I can tell you, there were tears and dramas in the middle of the night. I couldn't cope. But David said, "Look—you want to be an actress. My passion is horses and polo. And it is the you who is passionate about what you do that I love."

"And I wouldn't want you to be a tame husband," I said, "and I'm proud of my children's resilience."

The next day I stopped desperately trying to get Katie's and the baby's attention and I went off with David to a polo match and ate potato chips, and watched, and was the wife. I dressed Katie in the morning, took her to school, didn't do anything special, just got quietly back into the life, and in the evening I talked to Katie about what I'd been doing, and about the little orphan

RIGHT: *Attempting to play polo with David. If you can't beat them, join them!*

BELOW: *Feeding Katie for* Vogue *shoot in Arizona.*

who plays my son in the series. She wanted to buy him a present from her, so we went out and bought one. Suddenly everything was all right, because I had relaxed, been passive, listened to Katie, listened to David, been receptive to their needs.

There have been many times in my life when I have been too active, too busy trying. Make sure that you are able to accomplish the transition from busy, successful, struggling woman to the other kind of woman, the kind who is understanding and warm. That woman, who is also part of you, is equally extraordinary.

Many of my heroines aren't famous; they're friends of mine, in Los Angeles and in England, who live their lives well. Some are old friends, dating from far back before I became a film star; others I met when following the Jane Fonda pregnancy workout course. Some manage a career as well as children, some devote themselves to their children, remaining calm and being marvelous mothers and wives.

You have all kinds of potential inside you. Perhaps you have the potential to be a great writer like Colette. Perhaps you have the potential to be a great cook. Perhaps you could be a pianist. Or perhaps you could be a marvelous wife and mother. Learn from your heroines—bring their brilliance into your life.

Discover all these figures that lurk inside you, waiting for you to find the key to unlock them. Sometimes reading about your heroines or heroes can help to unlock these prisoners inside you. You mustn't just read about Colette and think, Gosh, what an amazing woman; I wish I could be like that, and then do nothing about it. You must make the connections. Ask ques-

As Colette, my romantic heroine.

tions. *How* could I be like that, even just a little like that? How can I convert my life into hers? How can I be like her? What lessons are there for me from her life? Don't just admire from afar. When you watch television, don't just dreamily stare at the scene in which a couple make love by the fireside: instead, make love by the fireside. Don't live your life at secondhand. Live it firsthand, in the present, and live it well. Let the television and the films inspire you, give you ideas to make your life extraordinary however ordinary it might seem to others.

If in your heart of hearts you see yourself as a splendid horsewoman, learn to ride. And don't put off taking the lessons for a month or two—start now. It's not difficult. And once you've learned, you'll find that there is nothing quite as romantic as riding through the fields at dawn, at dusk, with the wind in your face and the ordinary world speeded up by the speed of your horse and the thump of your heart.

Courage is what I'm arguing for, the courage to be both adventurous and feminine, to remain vulnerable and yet to be courageous too, to live an ordinary life in an extraordinary way. One of my heroines is Katharine Hepburn's character in *The African Queen.* When I'm in a physically dangerous situation I remember her. For instance, I'm terrified of flying. But I was once involved with someone who liked flying, and I actually let him teach me to fly. That helped me overcome my fear of flying and enabled me to share the exhilaration he experienced.

You don't have to attempt a replica of the life of your heroine: just add some aspects of her extraordinary life to your life. You might change your life in ways few

My fantasy as a horsewoman, riding my favorite horse, James; with Stacey our groom.

other people would notice. But you'll notice. You'll see better, hear better, find a new quality to living, a new way of loving.

Ballerinas were my heroines as a child. I started going to the local ballet school when I was tiny. Because of my knee injury I didn't achieve my dream of becoming a ballerina—oh, I danced in Festival Hall, I attended a full-time ballet school, I tried to become Margot Fonteyn—but I incorporate dancing into my everyday life. It doesn't matter that I'm not onstage at Covent Garden, that I'm not out there in that other, fairy-tale world of lost loves, of graceful movements, of dying swans, of satin and lace, of witches and princesses. Whenever I see a large space, I dance. Dancing is a physical way of expressing yourself. It's feeling something inside and expressing it without the use of words. And it's a very sensual, sexy way of communicating with your body. I dance barefoot or I put on my toe or tap shoes. I dance all by myself, or with my daughter, Katie, or with my mother and sisters, whoever happens to be visiting. We dance either in the huge empty ballroom of the house in England or on the grassy lawns outside. And wherever I go I take my toe shoes, carefully stuffed with potpourri. They were my dream and my reality for such a long time it is hard to renounce them.

Anyone who has a lawn can be a prima ballerina. Anyone can be Margot Fonteyn. Don't gawp at those who seem to you to live extraordinary lives. That's not the way. Learn what you can from the qualities they have instead of envying their happiness or successes. Take those qualities into your own life. Try to be a better person, a happier person. And if you envy them their ability to dance and are ashamed of your inability, just dance while no one is looking, and then you can be the best ballerina in the world. Or act. When no one's around, act out plays in front of the mirror just as you did when you were a child. So you'll never be the best actress in the world—but no one will know. If you're brave enough you can join an amateur acting club.

Follow your passions. Don't think that to be happy you have to be famous or publicly successful. That's another trap of our society, which worships success. The most successful person in the world is probably someone nobody has ever heard of; he or she has lived her life well, with happiness, dignity, imagination. Now *that* is an extraordinary life. As pressure on families and relationships increases, there is even more reason for people to learn how to live, rather than just learn how to work. Life is not only your accomplishments; it's what you do in your private life when there is no one to applaud you. You don't have to build a business empire or be a great artist to be immortal. You pass on a way of life to your children. You can bequeath them happiness and a sense of proportion and a capacity to be romantic. Remember that romance doesn't just mean men and sex; it is a way of looking at life, a way of living, of being happy and special.

One of my happiest moments, which put everything in proportion, was during the premiere of the James Bond film *Live and Let Die*, when I was meeting the Queen. I was very tense, worried about whether I would look good, if I would behave properly, how the film would be received. Then, at the back of a crowd

British Academy of Film and Television Awards, 1984, *with my proud father.*

at the bottom of some steps, I saw my father, nodding his head, saying just from the look on his face that he was proud of me, that he didn't want to disturb me, but that he was there. I realized that none of the glitter mattered to him and instantly it no longer mattered to me.

Private life, private moments, are what matter. Public life is of small consequence compared to private happiness.

If you feel that the world's grown dull, that you can't see anything marvelous, just get up very early one day and walk through the familiar streets you thought were so dull. You'll see they are transformed—suddenly they are strange, magical, mysterious: the dull dry-cleaning shop suddenly looks distinctly odd, the coffee shop is different now it's empty. And the air feels different, fresher, newer, as it renews you.

Don't obey the rules. Don't get up when everyone else gets up. If you want to keep all those other, marvelous, selves inside you prisoners, then do as you've always done and as everyone else does. But if you want to free them, you have to free yourself, change your pattern, jolt the old, familiar things into new, unfamiliar things.

If there's a window near where you're reading this, look out of it. Really look. Observe. Look at the colors, the movement of the wind, the shape of things. If you look long and hard enough you'll see a new world just outside your window.

You don't have to go to the ends of the world to find the miraculous: the miraculous is right outside your window if you only look. And it's right inside your heart.

4

Thinking Romantically

Iɴ this book I'm talking to everyone, because everyone has the potential to be happy, fulfilled, romantic, and beautiful. Beauty doesn't come just from the pleasant arrangement of features on a face; it comes from an inner peace and an enthusiasm for life.

It's easy to write that. It is much more difficult to overcome the problems and bad ways of thinking and feeling that stand in the way of happiness and romance.

The old view of God and the Devil arguing it out up in your brain whenever you are deciding between a good action and a bad action isn't too far from the truth, is it, really? I'm constantly struggling not to be envious if some actress gets a part I wanted. But if you want to be the romantic heroine of your imagination it just won't do for you to be thinking grisly, murderous thoughts about the woman in the house next door or the actress who has your part. If you are going to have the time to live a rich, fulfilled life, filling it with beauty and romance, as well as a successful working life, you just have to learn to control your bad emotions.

And bad they are. I am fed up with the modern view that everything unpleasant in your brain is someone else's fault—your father's, your mother's, whoever's. Bad emotions are bad and should be controlled—whoever's fault they might be. Instead of going to an analyst and finding out whose fault it is that you find yourself loathing the woman down the road, just spend that time and effort concentrating on controlling those negative emotions. Don't respect the negative emotions. Tell them to get lost. Or learn to keep them in their place. Some of them are old friends—old familiar demons—and life would be empty without their occasional appearance, but they must not be allowed to run the show. As Shakespeare points out: "There is nothing either good or bad, but thinking makes it so."

Here are some of the weapons I use to fight off the negative emotions and attitudes that can give you sleepless, unromantic nights and unpleasant lines of anger on your face. Not that I always succeed. But I'm not going to dwell on the times I failed. This book would be very dull if it droned on about my failures.

First, you must face up to problems and deal with them. That is the positive, romantic way. Do not allow time and temper to be sandpapered away by friction. There is no time for wasteful thoughts and anger.

If you are upset, talk about it, and having talked

about it, forget it. Whenever I don't get a role I want or if I get bad reviews, I feel it's an absolute disaster. I cry; I decide it's because people don't like me: I feel sorry for myself and I get angry with myself for feeling that way. But it only lasts for a short time. I cry and the anger goes away. It is necessary to express grief, anger, envy. But after you've expressed them, dismiss them—don't let them hang around ruining your life.

We have what are probably the usual problems with an extended family: David was married before and has a child by his first wife. At first Lynda, his first wife, and I did not get on. We didn't know each other at all, but eventually we met and discussed everything. She said the problem was that she couldn't talk to David, and I said, "Okay—talk to me then. We'll be friends." Now we are friends, and her daughter, Jenni, is a real sister to our daughter, Katie. It was just a matter of talking it out, of each person trying to understand the other's needs and points of view.

We all at some time get trapped in our own little worlds, our own little selfish prison of grievances and anger. We don't see anything but our own point of view. How can you be romantic if you're bitter and miserable? That's why talking is important. It helps you to understand what is going on in another person's mind—to understand their grievances.

Next, it is essential to think positively and to remember that the anger happens inside you. If you are angry with someone, it is your anger, not their behavior, that is upsetting you. Once you have talked it out and if there still seems to be no solution, just shelve the anger. Why bother with it? Why make whatever wrong was done to you worse by worrying over it? Just chuck

David laughing with his girls, Jenni and Katie.

it out with the garbage. Learn to control it.

After all, in a busy, romantic life there is simply not the time to waste. You have only one life. Live it, enjoy it, don't let bad feelings and wasteful ways of thinking fill your days when you should be kicking through fallen leaves, watching the waves come in, biting into an apple on a crisp autumn day. In my job I travel a great deal, all over the world, and I have to tell you: It is a very beautiful world.

Briefly, if you can do something about a problem, do it, and if there's nothing you can do about it, why on earth spend time worrying about it? For instance, I have learned to accept my failings, to realize they're part of me. I think everyone is anxious about at least some part of her body. Some hate their arms, some their hips; one woman I know of is horribly embarrassed by her knees. In the film business you are, of course, supposed to be body perfect. Since I've had my babies, my breasts have become even smaller than they were, but I make a joke about it. During scenes in *Crossings* I would simply say, "With or without breasts?" and if they wanted breasts, I'd turn around and pop in some padding. Also, I'm only five feet four, and my leading men all tend to be much taller. I think nothing of jumping on a box to make me taller.

I know I'm not particularly tall and I haven't got big breasts, but why should I worry about that which I can't change? It's me. If you think you've got a big nose or if you feel fat, just don't concentrate on those features. Look at your best features and accentuate them. If your eyes are nice, accentuate your eyes, always make them up well. My long hair is one of my best features, so I make the most of it and wash and condition it every day.

Each time I come across a problem I ask myself, "Can I do anything about it? If not, why worry about it?"

With my husband's help I run our Tudor house in England, our modern house in Los Angeles, and the one we rent in Santa Barbara. Inevitably, we have occasional problems with staff. The manager of our house in England some time ago suddenly quit and sold a hurtful, manufactured story to a newspaper. Hurtful stories often turn up in the papers and on film sets. I have only to look at another man and an invented romance gets reported back to David! Of course, this kind of thing is hard to cope with. But you have to. Force yourself to ignore it; then it doesn't hurt you. As far as you're concerned it needn't have happened. When the stories are untrue and damage your reputation, of course, you have to try to stop them from happening again. But I try never to lose sleep over the malice of others. Why bother? There really is no point, nothing to be gained.

Sometimes I do get upset about my faults. I dislike the way I speak before I think. I'm always saying the wrong thing at the wrong time. If David tells me not to talk about a particular subject, for instance, I always talk about it. If I'm with a homosexual actor, I'll find myself talking about AIDS.

Another major fault of mine is to talk about myself too much. David teases me about this. "Yes, darling," he says, "I'd love to know more about your career."

I try not to behave like this. But it keeps happening, so all I can do is have a sense of humor about it, and laugh at myself. If you laugh at yourself, nobody can sneer at you—it's called the "Head-them-off-at-the-pass technique."

A sense of humor is a great savior.

I remember an occasion when a very wealthy couple came to lunch with us at St. Catherine's Court, our house in England. We were trying to impress them with its beauty and had planned a meal that the cook was organizing. As we walked about the grounds before lunch, and David was asking me what we were going to eat, all of a sudden we heard some very rude words from the kitchen, followed by the sight of a blackened quiche being hurled out the window.

We tried to direct our guests' attention to some birds in the sky.

Nobody can do everything well. Laugh about your disasters and failings—get them in proportion.

There are other helpful ways of thinking that I want to share with you—one made famous by the Chinese philosopher Confucius, who wrote: "When you have a problem climb up onto a star, and look down on the world and see the insignificance of your trouble." He is telling us not to get our own small problems out of proportion. If we put anything in context, in the context of time and the immensity and beauty of space and earth, the problem immediately dwindles to nothing. We are part of the beauty of everything. We belong here. But we are really very small, and our problems even smaller. So when everything is too much for you, just climb onto a star and look down, and suddenly, as if by magic, all the muddle will clear.

Fear doesn't always go away quite so easily, and to be romantic it is essential to be brave, to be daring. Romance is risky. It is romantic to climb mountains, to ski fast down a dangerous slope, to run away to live alone on a distant island. Romance is about changing normal perspectives, about reaching new states of mind and feeling, about taking risks. It is seldom the easy way out. But romance is also about being vulnerable, about laying yourself open to new experience, about being open and receptive enough to enjoy your family, to enjoy nature, to enjoy loving and being loved. And while this, too, is risky, the rewards are great.

My life has been a series of risks. It was risky to become a ballet dancer, it was risky to become an actress. These were not safe, familiar, predictable ways of life. It was risky to head off for Hollywood again, (my first venture there was a miserable experience), with no money, in the hope of finding work. And life when I first arrived there was risky too. I found an apartment only because the girl in front of me in the supermarket queue chatted with me and happened to mention she was leaving hers. I had little money. I had to make everything last. I would buy just a few perfect strawberries and eat them out in my little garden, my paradise. I kept thinking I'd have to return home. And all the time, I was, without knowing it, risking my relationship with the man who was to be my second husband, Geep Planer. He was English, and had intended to come and live with me in Los Angeles—indeed, it was he who had encouraged me to go back to Hollywood to make my fortune. But when he came to visit, he found he hated Los Angeles. On a short visit back in England, where I was filming *The Four Feathers*, we got married, in a desperate bid to keep our love, but it was hopeless.

Taking risks can take you to great happiness, but it

can also bring you sadness.

One of the biggest risks David and I have taken is buying our large house in England, near Bath, a vast place designed to eat up time and money, over five thousand miles from home. It isn't a reasonable investment—although, in a way, perhaps it is, because it's an investment in what matters most of all: life and happiness.

No one in their right mind would have bought this rambling, broken-down Tudor mansion. But we did. We saw it, and saw in our imaginations what it could be like, and decided to buy it whatever the trouble and cost. And there has been plenty of trouble and cost, but it has all been worth it.

I first entered through its magnificent doors when I was filming a scene from Daphne du Maurier's *Jamaica Inn* there. David came round at lunchtime the first day of filming, and I could see he was smitten by the place, too. At that time we had no idea it was for sale.

"It's amazing," I said, looking at him hard.

He read my mind.

"We can do it. Why not?" (One of David's great gifts is his positive way of thinking. It is why he is a first-class businessman. He is not afraid of gambles.)

And the gamble was worth it. The house gives us more satisfaction, more joy and happiness than anything else. Whenever I earn any money I say, "Great! That's the tapestry," or "Marvelous. That's the dining-room table," or "There goes the dry rot and the death-watch beetle."

It was Bertrand Russell who said that the way he dealt with fear was to consider "seriously and deliber-

*David carrying me over the threshold the day we bought
St. Catherine's Court—our "romantic folly."*

ately" the worst that could happen in any risky situation. Then he said, "Having looked this possible misfortune in the face, give yourself sound reasons for thinking that after all it wouldn't be such a terrible disaster. Such reasons always exist, since at the worst nothing that has happened to oneself has any cosmic importance . . . you will find your worry diminishes to a quite extraordinary extent."

You can't live your life crouching in corners, afraid of everything. You have to dare. Of course, as you grow older, and once you have children, it is harder to do so because you are risking the happiness of vulnerable children, of other people who need you. If you die mountaineering or move to live in a desert to follow your romantic notion about living like a Bedouin, it will be they who suffer. When you have young children, they need security and, at least for a while, a steady life, filled with a sense of romantic living. For them, it is exciting and dangerous to climb along a wall with you there to catch them. This is the time for sharing their romantic view of the world, not for egotistically following your own desires.

What many people fear most of all is failure. And of course you need never fail at anything if you never do anything. Except that in that case you fail at life.

What I tell myself when I fail is that I have done my best. That is what prevents me fearing failure. I feel I can only do my best. You have to do your own best, not someone else's best. And not necessarily better than anyone else. But if you do less than your best, then you will always be upset with yourself.

The person who taught me that principle of romantic life was not Confucius, or Bertrand Russell,

St. Catherine's in winter.

Running on the surf at Santa Barbara with Jenni and Katie.

but my mother!

It is not possible to do everything well. You just have to do your best. You don't have to drive yourself into a mental breakdown by trying to be perfect: a marvelous cook, a brilliant wife, the best possible mother, a sparkling hostess, a top businesswoman. How can you? Fail at some things. So what? Often I don't look as good as I should or entertain as well as I'd like to. But I just say to myself, "Well—this is me." And if people are interested in me, this is the real me, not a pretend or fake me that has been carved and painted and porcelained. My nails are invariably cracked. I am not Supermom and Supercook: I have to have nannies to help me look after my children, and I have a cook to help me prepare the family's food. I'm not ashamed of that. I do my best and as much as I can.

Every mother feels guilty at times if she works outside the home, away from her children. But once you have made the decision not to be a full-time mother, stop feeling guilty. You decided to work because you had to or knew you'd be miserable if you didn't, and what use is a miserable mother to any child?

Have an upbeat attitude toward your work and your children. Don't allow your responsibilities to grind you down. Enjoy yourself. Make sure that you don't live in order to work, but work in order to live. Make time to enjoy your marriage and your children and yourself. Dare to have the occasional decadent weekend away with your husband, have the occasional self-indulgent lunch all by yourself in a grand restaurant with a marvelous book, take the children off to the beach and watch how well they know how to take pleasure from life.

Don't always put the children first, or always put your work first, or always put your husband above everything. Order your priorities to fit changing circumstances: be flexible and open.

But if you want everything—marriage and children and work—and you don't want to be worn down into a world-weary, haggard creature, you have to learn to delegate, to let other people have the glory for some aspects of your life.

I have had some marvelous nannies. Bianca, my present one, sends Katie and Sean out to meet me as I come down from the airplane, and Katie is holding a flower to give me. I love to be met at airports. A friend of mine recently arrived at an airport and saw no one there to meet her, no car, nobody. There was only a limousine there, and she knew it wasn't for her. But her lover was hiding in the back of the chauffeur-driven car with a bottle of champagne. It is that kind of action that makes life worthwhile and makes one able to cope with all the problems, all the trials, all the difficulties.

It is petty and unreasonable to try to do everything yourself if you can afford to have help. But remember to treat whomever you hire with respect: don't denigrate their work because you feel you're a failure as a woman for needing their help. Be romantic, be positive, and be kind.

You have to make a decision to let someone else have a proper relationship with your children. You can't always be interrupting the nanny when she's playing with them, when things are going well, to demand that they come shopping with you or that they sit while you read to them. You have to choose someone who has the same attitudes as you do, and then let them get to work. It is essential not to diminish their relationship. If you do, it's bad for the children, and bad for you.

Choose someone warm and romantic and loving. Treat her well. The art of delegation is the art of mixing firmness with kindness. It is an error to grow so close to your nanny that you find it hard to give her instructions. You must respect her, and her job, and she must respect you, and your job. Your children should be encouraged to love you both and respect you both.

A good nanny will make sure that the most important relationship is with you. The best ones have a way of vanishing at the right times, and appearing at the right times.

And when things go wrong—when the nanny walks out, when it's her day off and you have to work—don't panic. Always keep calm. Sometimes my mind goes berserk and I think: I can't do it all. I have to go away. How will my children cope without me? Who will run the house? I don't know my part yet. I've got an interview today and some photographs and I look awful. Panic.

The way to avert panic in any situation—in a painful childbirth as much as on a busy day—is simply to take one thing at a time and concentrate fully upon it. That is the romantic way. Would Shelley have written his great romantic poetry if he had been fretting about where to buy a cutlery set? Did Isadora Duncan worry about buying broad beans while dancing? It is essential to deal with each problem separately, to take things one at a time.

If I do one thing at a time, I can handle all my responsibilities: wife to David; mother to Katie and

Sean; stepmother to David's child, Jenni; film producer; film star; actress; manager of three houses; chairperson for a charity, RP Foundation, which fights blindness; promoter of Le Jardin, the Max Factor perfume.

Each problem is only one problem, after all.

I believe that if you do something wholeheartedly, with a positive approach, and give that one thing your full attention, you can do pretty well anything in life.

From the time I was a small girl I have had a habit of becoming obsessed with things, becoming totally involved. The image of a romantic is of someone vague and airy-fairy. Real romantics aren't like that. They concentrate hard on what they are doing while they are doing it. This ability to become absorbed in whatever I am doing helps my acting. When I'm acting, I become the character I'm playing. Kathy in *East of Eden* was a very depressing role. It was hard to escape from the part and return to ordinary life, even after we had finished filming. I felt schizophrenic, like Kathy, and I began to feel her arthritis in my own joints. But if I hadn't become obsessed, I couldn't have played the part convincingly. It's the same with anything you do. You have to throw yourself into whatever you do, whether it's having a party, organizing a business deal, designing a dress. That is the way to avoid panic. That is the way to live a rich, full life.

When I'm acting, I time-walk myself out of everything that is happening in my life, every distraction, and find myself in another place. I have to be sure not to be terribly rude to people at the same time. This ability to be somewhere else is a great help even in ordinary life. When things become too much, and panic sets in, and none of your mental tricks work, try this one: Try to time-walk (daydream is another word for it) yourself away from the here and now. Drift away, mentally fly away, to a beach, to the sea, to somewhere peaceful, just for a while, to give your overworked brain a holiday.

David summons me back from these trips on the flying carpet of my mind with the words "Earth to Jane. Can you read me? Can you read me?" He says that when I'm daydreaming he has no idea where I might be, but it's most certainly not on earth! Romantics are never quite on earth: they have the ability to create heaven on earth, to float away from the here and now when it all presses in too much.

When you're feeling overwrought and you need a lift, you could also drink a glass of champagne, buy some flowers, listen to your favorite music, anything special that makes you feel better about your life.

I know I can make David's day by suddenly bringing home some oysters. My special treats are pistachios and pickled gherkins. The husband of a friend of mine loves figs, and when he's going away she sometimes secretes a packet of figs somewhere in his bag, so he will find them when he unpacks.

If a man puts a red rose next to your bed, or some chocolates on the pillow, that can give you a big lift. But why wait until you're spending a weekend away? Why wait until a much-planned grand occasion? Treat yourself, and treat your partner. *There is nothing stopping you* from elevating the ordinary with a little imagination, a little thought, a little flair. When I was filming *War and Remembrance* in Yugoslavia and Poland I noted how people brought flowers with them whenever they went out with friends for drinks or dinner or for no particular reason. It's an old European custom that used to be more prevalent, in England in particular, than it is now.

I actually believe in an emergency kit: candles, a bottle of fizzy wine or champagne, and some lumpfish roe or caviar should always be kept available to make an occasion of an ordinary day. For that is what romance is; it's making occasions out of every ordinary day of your life, turning each one into something special.

MOVIE STILLS

Tom Selleck and I in Lassiter.

BELOW LEFT: Seventh Avenue.

BELOW RIGHT: The Sun Also Rises.

Mary Yellen—romantic heroine from Jamaica Inn.

Marguerite in The Scarlet Pimpernel.

Oh! What a Lovely War—*disguised as a blonde. My first film role, at the age of seventeen.*

Crossings—*Hilary.*

5

Strong and Feminine: The Romantic Woman

THIS is not just a book about how to find and keep the love of your life. It is about how to be a romantic person. Once you are that person, I believe that what you want most in life will be yours. And if what you want is the person who will be the love of your life, I have no doubt you'll find him or her.

Men as much as women should try to find their romantic selves.

The idea of chivalry is not just a matter of men opening doors for women and thereby charming them. When it flourished in the fourteenth and fifteenth centuries it was based on a certain code of values, in particular the idea of honor, and of respect for the femininity of women and the vulnerability of children.

This notion of respect matters a great deal. If you are to live a romantic, happy life you must respect others. You are on this planet with other people, sharing it with other people, and you must treat them well. You must listen to them, care for them, try to understand them. And they will do the same for you: the smile that you send out returns to you.

What I'm saying in this book combines the two meanings of the word *romance:* romance as in Romantic, the ambitious, striving, self-based philosophy of the great nineteenth-century writers, and romance as in the more conventional sense of sharing, finding love, and perhaps marrying and starting a family. This combination is also a fusion of the two great strands in a twentieth-century woman's life: the Romantic philosophy of feminism, having to do with finding your individual self and developing it, and the older, more traditional and often insistent need for love and beauty and a family, without which many women feel their lives negated.

You can have both. It doesn't have to be one or the other. You can be successful in your career *and* you can be feminine, maternal, loving, but to do so you must respect romance. You must not move, lock, stock, and barrel, into that gray male world of offices and telephones, because if you do so you are in danger of forfeiting what there is in you that is essentially feminine. If you are a woman why not use feminine wiles sometimes? Why not dress your talents in charm. Charm will open more doors than knocking them on the head will.

Don't be afraid of dressing to suit your own tastes—

and don't be afraid of flirting. Don't think that men won't treat you seriously if you flirt. They must learn that women must be true to their own natures. That is the next revolution, that is the romantic revolution I'm searching for.

Flirting is a way of bringing someone close to you, of sharing a mood. It is a harmless, delightful game two people can play, and by learning to flirt, you can create romantic moments wherever you are.

Flirting isn't just sexual behavior: it's part of a sensual and emotional way of behaving toward other people that flatters and interests them. It's the way you look at a man across the table, listen to him, and make him smile and laugh. It's a way of reminding him that all is not dull and standardized and unisex yet. Fluttering your eyelashes isn't good flirting: listening with intelligence and interest is the way that romantic, twentieth-century women flirt.

Of course, flirting has to be handled with care. Inspired by the example of Scarlett O'Hara, I used to test my ability to flirt, and once, on holiday with some friends, I flirted with my best friend's boyfriend. I learned the power I had. She never quite forgave me. And to this day I am not proud of that action.

It took me a long time to have the confidence to be my feminine self—to be both strong and feminine. To be each was easy; to combine them was the problem. It was only when I came to terms with who I really was that I found a happy, stable marriage. For me, as for so many, it was hard to combine the two meanings of the word *romantic*—the search for self, and the sharing. It was only when I found myself that I could share.

Max Factor's ad for Le Jardin fragrance—the profusion of flowers enhances the romantic mood.

There is a lesson here, I think, for all women who want to be strong *and* feminine. Learn from my mistakes. First of all, learn to be your own person. Learn to be alone sometimes. Build up your strong, romantic self. Then you will have the strength to cope with the demands of marriage and children as well as all the demands of being a woman in the twentieth century; of being expected to have a career, or a job, or at least some impressive talents.

Don't rush into marriage and children before you are ready for them. Grow up a bit, grow strong, take risks, and then marry when you are strong enough to share, to be occasionally selfless, to love someone else as much as yourself. But first you have to learn to love yourself, and know yourself.

Like so many women, I spent my teenage years and my twenties trying to be what other people wanted me to be. It's fine to be what other people want you to be, so long as you have a firm hold on who you *really* are. I didn't.

When I met my first husband, Michael Attenborough, I was very impressed by his intelligence and his authority. To please him I tried to become an intellectual. I read books on Marx and Lenin. Oh, I tried to be very serious. When he was a student at Sussex University, I stayed with him there, and discussed politics and literature with him and his friends. I always felt inadequate, because, I realize now, I was trying to be him. But of course I could never be him. We were very different personalities with very different brains. How could I have been so stupid?

He took control of everything. I might have known that would be the case after our first meeting, on

Brighton Pier, during the filming of *Oh! What a Lovely War*, which Michael's father, Richard Attenborough, directed.

I was only seventeen, and stood with the other girls playing the chorus. Plastered with make-up, my eyelashes smothered in mascara, I thought I resembled an old hooker.

A freckly, stocky, very attractive young man came up to me and asked did I like the theater and did I have a diary. I handed him my diary, and he proceeded to fill it in for four weeks, three shows a week.

"What are you doing?" I said.

"I've got tickets for today, tomorrow, next week, the week after . . ." he said, confirming this commitment by pulling all the tickets out of his wallet. It was so romantic!

From then on, we were inseparable, and three years later we were married.

It was only while I was away in Jamaica filming my part as Solitaire in *Live and Let Die* that I began to think about our relationship. I was playing the little woman in my life with Michael. I was playing the part I thought Michael wanted me to play.

The director of *Our Mutual Friend*, a television series based on the Dickens novel, later told me, "You have to be your own woman." I didn't understand what he meant. It tortured me that I didn't know what he meant.

It has been the hardest lesson for me to learn, to become my own woman. I had been a little girl for my parents, a little woman for the man in my life, a ballerina for my teachers, an actress for directors and producers, a wicked smoldering sex goddess for some

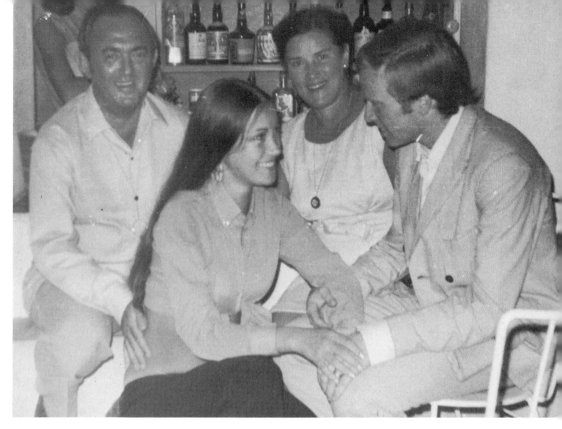

Romantic summer holiday in Spain with Michael Attenborough and my parents. Age seventeen.

Premiere of Live and Let Die *with Roger Moore, Michael Attenborough, and Princess Anne.*

journalists, a virginal creature for others. I had wanted to please everyone.

There's a simple realization, which didn't come until much later for me, but I'll share it with you now. It's a realization that is crucial to anyone's happiness and self-respect: *You* matter. Find out who you are; don't try to be someone for everyone. The only way to please everyone is simply to be yourself, a confident, affectionate, generous person. Your parents will probably be appalled when they see you growing into someone different from the dear little girl of their imaginations, but grow you must, and they'll respect and love you even more when they see that you have found your own way of life, your own way of living.

If you settle down too soon you'll resent your husband, as I did. It wasn't his fault. Neither of us was ready for the sharing and sacrifice that love and marriage demand. We were both too busy making our own way, finding out what we could do and what we couldn't, wanting excitement.

All the publicity over my landing the part of Solitaire in the famous Bond film *Live and Let Die* did not help our relationship either. Michael, who had been accustomed to being at the forefront of things as a talented young actor and director with a very famous father, was suddenly subjected to being the husband of a James Bond girl. And I was finding it hard to cope with the numerous different versions of me presented in the newspapers. I was beginning not to have any idea of who I was. I might have been a little confused before, but now I was really confused.

I was dressed by a top designer in expensive clothes, when my own taste was for homemade and sale clothes (admittedly due to a lack of funds). While preparing for the film, I discovered clothes for the first time. Everything was the best: I had shoes made to fit and underwear made of silk. I was amazed.

I should like to be able to say that my head was kept completely straight throughout—but it wasn't. Eventually I began to believe some of the things written about me, things that had been mostly made up by writers who were trying to make me more interesting.

One person in particular, a journalist and photographer, spent three days with me to find out who and what I was so that he could write an exclusive piece about the "sexy Jane Seymour." In desperation he begged me to tell him my fantasies. Did I like running through long grass, for example? I raised my eyebrows, wondering why I had to answer these questions. The next thing I knew, and without my control, an article appeared saying that I was a wild woman who loved running naked through long grass! Something, needless to say, I have never done—except perhaps when I was a toddler.

In the world of acting, even more than in the rest of life, you have to keep a tight hold on your identity if you don't want to go crazy. I didn't go crazy, but for a while I didn't know who I was and what was happening to me. I was being taken over by the media. I was even trying to live up to this manufactured person of their writers' imagination and behave more outrageously. I flirted more, wore sexier clothes. It was ridiculous.

Sometimes it is tempting to play the roles assigned to you by others. But it is dangerous. Always play the roles you want to play. Don't pretend to be something you're not, unless of course it's a fantasy you've decided upon. You don't belong to other people. You belong to yourself. What you are is all you have—everything around you can change—and it is important to develop that self and strengthen it. I suppose what I'm really talking about is your soul, your inner self. That must be your own. You can't be free and romantic until you know who you are. And you can't love another person properly until you know and love yourself.

I think I first began to see how foolish I was to let go of my own identity when I reported for my first day of work on the Bond set.

The producer took one look at me—with the designer clothes, make-up, hair, everything—and said, "You look dreadful."

"*I* think I look dreadful, too. But this is what I was told you wanted."

"You looked better when you came to my office."

"Well, that's the way I dress, that's the way I really am," I said.

From then on, when it came to clothes, I made a point of wearing only what I thought right for me and for the character I was playing. I became involved in dress designing, and showed the costume designers what I liked and what I thought would work on me. A character and its clothes have to be part reality. They have to be based on you. This was how my infamous wardrobe began.

It's the same for life outside the world of acting: you must always follow your own tastes. If you wear only what other people think looks good, if you wear the latest fashion just because it is the latest fashion, you won't be comfortable, and therefore you won't look good. Beauty comes from being content with your body, with your mind, with your clothes, and with your face. Your clothes should express you, bring out the qualities in you, help you to be yourself. You should discover what is romantic for you, not just copy the looks of others. Wear veils, wear white, wear hats, wear your hair in a way that is special to you. Find out what you look marvelous in, and what suits your life, and wear it. You may surprise yourself and love the changes. Find a sense of humor to suit your style.

* * *

During this filming, it was as if I were leaving home for the first time. I had to make my own decisions and to stand up for myself. The great thing was that I discovered that I could. Until then, I had relied on Michael to make all my decisions for me. Now I realized I was capable of standing up for myself and it wasn't fair of me to put him in that position.

One day, before we started filming in New Orleans, I went to Bourbon Street to visit a tarot card reader. I thought I should watch her technique to help me with my part as Solitaire. I had taken off my wedding ring. She knew nothing about me. I was just a stranger off the street. But she told me things that were destructive to my life, destructive because I half believed them.

She told me I would be married three times.

It was the most horrible piece of information I could have been told. My parents had been married for so long, so happily. I believed in marriage. I believed that marriage is forever.

But I had had misgivings the night before I married, that deep down inside me I was role playing. I was trying to be someone for my husband-to-be that wasn't me. I wasn't sure how long I could keep up this role. Of course it was too late; the caterers were cooking, the invitations had been answered. . . .

After my return from the set of *Live and Let Die*, Michael and I drifted apart. Eventually we discussed what we wanted to do—to be separate from one another, or to live together—and we found we were actually happier living apart.

In a way, the Bond film broke up our marriage . . . or perhaps it was the tarot cards. All the same, I don't regret that film. I look forward to the day when my children's children will ask, "Granny, what did you do while you were growing up?" and I'll be able to show them a picture of me as Solitaire, tied to a stake and looking very sexy and wild . . . my wild, misspent youth.

I was still developing, testing, trying to find out who I might be, what I could do, what I wanted. The last person I needed was someone who took me over, and the last person Michael needed was someone as restless as I. Although he appeared very confident, and took charge of everything, he hadn't found himself any more than I had. We simply had not had the time.

So do as I say, not as I did, and grow up before marrying. Fortunately, I had no children in my two failed marriages. I am thankful for that.

But even after the agony of my breakup with Michael, the feminine side of my character wanted to settle down again, to have the security of a steady relationship with a man. I still couldn't cope on my own. I still wasn't my own woman.

I fell in love with Geep Planer, an old friend of Michael's. After an unsuccessful foray to America, where

I was subjected to the casting-couch routine, I subsided into domesticity with Geep.

It all seemed perfect. Geep is one of the sweetest, funniest, most romantic men in the world, a businessman and brilliant cartoonist. Far less egotistical about his career than Michael and I, he always had my interests at heart, and I loved him dearly. But oddly enough, it is Michael I see now. I suppose Michael and I are alike, and that is why we loved each other, and that is why we broke up, and that is why we are good friends now. Geep is gentler, and I think we hurt each other more.

I am explaining about my marriages at some length so that you can learn from my mistakes, and perhaps marry the right man the first time, instead of the third time, like me! Also, I want to warn you not to take the romantic side of your nature to extremes. People think it is the sign of a hardened, unromantic person to marry more than once. Quite the opposite. It is usually the sign of a romantic, someone who loves to fall in love and follow the whole dream to its conclusion. Of course the romance and the wedding and the honeymoon are all marvelous. But don't get too carried away. Temper your romanticism with good sense.

I shouldn't have settled down with Geep until I had cured that restless side of me that was seeking new challenges, new discoveries about myself. And I certainly wasn't ready for another marriage.

While with Geep I embroidered blouses for Brown's, one of London's top clothing shops. I saw myself as a sweet, domestic creature. Then I was offered the part of Nora in Ibsen's *A Doll's House*, about a woman who walks out on her marriage in order to find herself. She is hemmed in, stifled, by the man who loves her and calls her funny little names.

It was a big success. And it reminded me, I'm afraid, that I, like Nora, was not ready for domesticity.

It was Geep who advised me to go and make my fortune in America. It was he who wanted me to take the risk—he was the brave one, I the coward. I went with no money on a six-week return ticket. But in the end I was the brave one. I stayed. Geep refused to join me permanently, as he had said he would. He hated Los Angeles and the film world. And although we married romantically, on the spur of the moment, it didn't work. I went off to my continent, and he stayed on his. Separated by distance, we soon grew more separate still.

Learn from my mistakes. I married two sweet, intelligent, romantic men before I was ready to be married. There is no doubt that romantics like me make many rash, hasty decisions. We want everything to be perfect, so we convince ourselves it is. We want an ideal, everlasting marriage, so we marry as soon as we can. We reach for the skies, but if you keep reaching for the skies you might just get there and leave your partner abandoned, earthbound.

Mix your romanticism with good sense. Try to have moments of realism.

I now have the sexiest, most mature, most affectionate marriage that I can imagine possible. Perhaps if you learn from my mistakes, you'll have just one, good, marriage. At all costs, marry as a grownup, not as a child.

At what stage did I grow up? I don't quite know. But I know that over the last few years I have become a calmer, stronger person than ever before. David recognized and loved the strength in me. He didn't want a fluttery little girl. He wanted a woman.

And when I met David, I had finally become a woman.

Some people are grown up at twenty, some not grown up at forty. It is not a matter of years but of personality and experience.

Become yourself before marrying someone else. It's not fair to anyone to enter into solemn vows if you are in a state of flux. Once you are confident of yourself, once you love yourself, once you are a grown woman instead of a girl, then you are capable of loving someone else with maturity and wisdom. Until then, in my experience, the love affairs should remain romance, and not develop into that deeper kind of romance called "marriage," especially if you mean to have children.

6

Keeping the Romance in Your Relationship

I N good, lasting relationships you don't stare into each other's eyes all the time: you look together in the same direction. You share life together.

The old advice about joining a club to meet people really is good advice. By sharing an activity—tennis, photography, beekeeping, whatever—you get to know and like another person.

Of course, sharing an adventure is the best way of all to fall in love. The adventures don't have to be dramatic ones, though. You could just wander into an old cinema and find that you're the only couple watching a film and it would be something about the emptiness and the atmosphere that drew you close, made the occasion special, strange, memorable.

Search out these special moments.

In England, I used to love to hire a boat on the Serpentine in Hyde Park and glide out onto the lake, suddenly transforming central London into the Amazon. I'd close my eyes, and the sounds of traffic, the cries of children, would drift far away and suddenly all there was in the entire world was me and the boyfriend who was with me. I'd dress for the occasion, with parasol and pretty dress, and take along a picnic.

If you want a special life, with special romance, don't be ordinary and predictable. Suggest a picnic—and if the weather is bad have it on the living-room floor. Suggest taking a boat out on the river or lake. Suggest a drive down to the beach one night. I was walking by the Thames in London recently and I was amazed at the number of couples standing kissing and talking by the waterside. Each one looked in love. There was a full moon; and the moon, and the dark restless river, and the couples belonged in a different, timeless London, far away from the traffic and the pubs and all those ordinary things.

Perhaps you are the kind of person just being with is an adventure—but most of us need the right settings and circumstances to flourish, to help bring out our romantic selves.

When life seems a little dull and run-of-the-mill, why not go to the airport, look at the schedule, and catch the first plane to wherever it's going? Or catch the first bus, or the first train. Take a gamble. Getting there—with a new boyfriend, a girlfriend, an old boyfriend, a husband—you can share an adventure. You might end up someplace that everyone considers dull; but your attitude will transform it. You'll wander around the place together, with no one knowing where you are, and the town or country will be somehow mysterious, magical. You'll find some little shop, or a museum with just one magnificent painting you never knew was there, or a superb restaurant in a back street. Whether the place you end up in is Minneapolis or Richmond, Virginia, or Tunbridge Wells, you'll find something there, and you'll never forget it.

It's that kind of gambling, of imaginative thinking, that gives drama to a relationship. And the odd thing is, it doesn't take money or much time; it simply takes the romantic attitude.

My second husband, Geep, loved spur-of-the-moment schemes—and one gloomy London day he saw some cheap air tickets advertised to Corfu. Within hours we were airborne.

On the plane it was announced that war had broken out in Corfu. No wonder someone didn't want those tickets! He said he wasn't at all afraid. But when I looked for the bread knife at the villa we rented, I found it under his pillow.

I'll never forget that holiday.

Those kinds of adventures are more fun and more romantic than going to the predictably "romantic" places, which lack the element of surprise. Sitting on a *bateau mouche* on the Seine in Paris and being presented with a red rose at a prearranged romantic meal with lots of other couples isn't that romantic. It's what is expected, and romance is about the unexpected. It's the unexpected, the exceptional, that can turn an ordinary relationship into an extraordinary one, that can make you suddenly fall in love. It's the moment when something goes wrong and you laugh—you share the moment of horror, and then the moment of laughter. It's when you settle down for a picnic and a horse approaches you and you look at each other and realize you're both terrified of horses. It's the moment before a thunderstorm, when the atmosphere is tense. It is sharing all those extraordinary moments in ordinary lives.

If you're in England, take a day trip across the Channel. Take the trip with your husband, or your boyfriend, or just a friend. Try fresh cheese from a market there, and experience that heaven of tasting perfect French cheese in the gentle sunlight of a market square, in the early morning after a trip across the water. It will cost you very little, and that day's adventure will refresh you, interest you, make you closer to your companion.

Wherever you live, go to farmers' markets and buy wine from vineyards, apples from orchards, milk from farms. Buy bagels, fill them with smoked salmon, eat them on a riverbank. Make an effort not to live a predictable, supermarket life, with everything prepackaged and prearranged.

Stint yourself sometimes on ordinary everyday things to afford the occasional luxury. It is the high points, the moments of luxury in an ordinary life—when you spend all your money on the best meal you've ever tasted, or one night in the town's best hotel—that are memorable. And when you look back on your life you will view its achievements in two ways: first, you will look at your achievements, public and private, and second, you will look back on the moment when you suddenly decided to open that bottle of champagne and drink it in the garden, or that moment when you both ran down the slope like children, laughing, with the sun on your faces and the wind in your hair. These moments matter.

Go to new places, do new things—never make do with the day-to-day.

My middle sister, Sally, actually met her husband, Michael, on an adventure when she was fifteen, when they were both on a school cruise to the Caribbean. Fifteen years later Michael's father, when they were moving, came across a box full of letters and gave them to Michael, who found that one of the letters was from Sally. Michael remembered her and phoned my parents' house (they hadn't moved). Sally happened to be there; they met, and it was love at second sight. But it was in part the memory of that shared happy trip that drew them close.

One reason our family is so close is that we shared so much together. In childhood our holidays were never planned. We'd set off sitting on top of suitcases and bed linens, with so many suitcases on the top of the car that I have no idea to this day how it ever moved, and with lettuce plants in the trunk to plant on arrival. (This was another of my mother's romantic gestures that made every place we went special. We'd plant the vegetables at the holiday cottage or wherever we ended up, and when they grew we'd have our own garden-fresh salad every day.) We'd do terrifically romantic things, like following the Rhine or the Danube and not knowing where we'd end up. We'd stop in a pension or a little hotel. We'd have picnics on the way, after stopping at a village shop and buying a loaf of bread and salami, which we'd eat somewhere beautiful, by a river or the sea, or in a field full of flowers.

Under mistletoe at Christmas, awaiting Katie, who was very late!

The three sisters on one of our adventurous vacations. In the Alps wearing the local dress.

My parents gave us so many memories of shared adventures that it is no surprise that we love them so much and are so close. It took a certain bravery on their part. Think of it: putting three small children into neither a new nor a very good car and hoping for the best as they set off for a destination unknown. We often used to end up in uncharted territory because my mother's map reading wasn't too good. But that was half the point of it. We were sharing our own, personal adventure, based on the personalities of those concerned: we weren't following someone's prearranged scheme. To this day, I dislike package tours as much as I dislike the whole package-tour mentality of life. We haven't been sold a life with a predictable beginning, middle, and end. We're all freewheeling adventurers in this world, and the more often you remind yourself of that, the better.

My father also shared his excitement about the world with us, as my mother did. They took us to castles on the Rhine and Danube, and told us all about them. In Holland he explained how windmills work, in Frankfurt he made sure we ate frankfurters. He treated life as an enchanting adventure, a magical mystery tour, and the sense of wonder he instilled in us has never left us.

If you have a similar sense of wonder, share it with others. And if you don't, find someone who will share theirs with you.

I met my husband David because we shared work together. Many couples meet that way. Little by little, by talking together, arguing together, they build up a mutual respect which turns to love.

I first met him at his office, where I had gone to

discuss the idea of his becoming my business manager. At that time his clients included Goldie Hawn, Paul Newman, and Warren Beatty. I thought that there was little chance he would take me on, because I wasn't in that league. But we had been recommended to each other by friends, so there was at least a possibility.

When I entered that office, he was in his gray pin-stripe suit, looking like a tall, dark-haired John Denver. He had an enormous banyan tree in the corner and, underneath it, a stuffed goose. And ducks every-where. Brass ducks, pictures of ducks, wooden ducks. Now bizarre as this might seem, in my little house in England I, too, had a tall banyan tree (which was very unusual in England, where we have only small potted plants), and ducks. I had a collection of ducks. Ducks everywhere. And the most surprising thing of all was that I, too, had a stuffed goose, one of those taxider-mist's numbers. Now how many people in the world have a stuffed goose? Actually, I was only minding mine for a friend, but it's still quite a coincidence. So I have to admit that it wasn't actually shared work that brought us together, but a mutual interest in ducks. At the time, I was missing England and my house there desperately and I felt at home in David's office, and with him, and with our shared interest in ducks.

Not romantic, admittedly not at all romantic. It isn't really a tip I'd pass on to anyone else. You could keep ducks in your office for a dozen lifetimes and never meet anyone who fell in love with you because of them!

He took me on. He says it was because I "looked nice." And, he says, "You were very eccentric and still are." (He may call me eccentric, but *he* was the one who kept that goose from choice.) I was wearing my little dirndl, my little frilly skirt, at a time when everyone else was wearing blue jeans.

We shared work together, and I also shared many of my secrets. As a client, I would have lunch with him to discuss where I was going with my career and what I wanted to do with my money. There was certainly an attraction between the two of us. But he always maintained he would never date a client, and I always maintained that I wouldn't mix business and pleasure. From running my financial life, he could tell a great deal about me; how I organized my life right down to how I spent my money and how I saved my money. He knew how much I spent on make-up, clothes, the hairdresser. All the idiosyncrasies were there on file.

He would ask me at lunch, "How come there are no expenses here for your household? None for housework, good general living?" I said, "It's very simple. I get invited out for breakfast, lunch, and dinner by different people." What I didn't say was that when I wasn't going out, I wouldn't eat, because I was always watching my diet. Or if I did, I'd eat virtually nothing. I would use chopsticks to make my food last longer.

I think David respected me when he saw that I ran my own life, and respect is crucial to a good relationship. If you don't respect the man or woman you're with, the relationship won't be happy. Make sure that you respect each other's work, the way the other behaves, and make sure you are respected. There is nothing more destructive than to be denigrated, and nothing more destructive than to denigrate. Mutual respect, mutual love; shared respect, shared love.

I certainly respected David and still do. He is a brilliant businessman, calm, responsible, and clever, and he has a talent for drama. In the early stages of our romance he kept me on my toes. When I left him in the morning, I never knew whether I would see him that evening. He used to leave it until three in the afternoon to phone. But one day we had a row and I decided to get away from him and Los Angeles. I phoned my agent, and found work in New York.

The next day when David phoned I wasn't there. I had gone to New York, where I had auditioned for a part in the theater, playing Mozart's wife in *Amadeus* on Broadway.

I was staying at the Hotel Pierre when David turned up. Joe Jackson was playing in Central Park that night, right under our window. There was a thunderstorm; we drank champagne. It was the most romantic evening of my life.

I think it was that evening, after missing each other so desperately, that we knew we would always be together.

There are lessons to be learned from all this: learn mutual respect, share your lives, but also make sure your life together doesn't get dull. Share drama and turmoil as well as quiet content. It is only through sharing high and low points together that you can get to know each other well, and know whether or not you really should be spending your lives together.

Occasionally test relationships: walk out on them if they're not right. If they're right after all, you will find each other again, with a surge of romance that will help you through duller, rainier days.

Keep a relationship developing, changing, alive.

I moved from the Hotel Pierre to a space-age loft in Soho, where, on Saturday nights, after two shows, I'd

Somewhere in Time *with Christopher Reeve—one of my favorite romantic roles.*

On the stage in Amadeus *after David proposed to me.*

cook for David. He'd fly in from Los Angeles and arrive about midnight, and I'd have arrived about ten to midnight, and at about half past midnight we'd be sitting down to a wonderful candlelit meal.

The separation gave a sense of drama to our relationship that has never left it.

We had known we were in love for a long while, and I suppose I was waiting, hoping for him to propose. He didn't go down on his knee. He did something rather better than that. He proposed to me one evening just before I was going onstage in *Amadeus*.

I do think proposals matter. A proposal is in a way the beginning of a marriage—it is setting the tone. If he asks you over breakfast or you have to ask him, it isn't a good sign. It is showing a lack of respect for life, for tradition, for the drama and fun and beauty of life, for romance.

In a way, a proposal is a means for you each to share that old drama of proposal and marriage, to enter into the world of fairy tale together.

Proposals matter. Valentines matter. It is by such rituals that we give form and substance to our lives and our love.

David is brilliant at breaking the pattern and behaving unpredictably and imaginatively. He knew exactly what time the curtain went up for *Amadeus* and exactly what time I went onstage to do my first scene, twenty minutes into the play. One night he waited until exactly five minutes before I had to go on, and then called me from Los Angeles and asked me to marry him, knowing that I would have to say yes or no because there would be no time to discuss the matter. I said yes.

Then I went onstage and whispered to Tim Curry, who played Mozart, "David has just asked me to marry him. . . ." And in the play it is at just that moment that Mozart proposes to me.

When Tim Curry cried, "Marry me!" I simply burst into tears.

FANTASY

While writing this book I was inspired to indulge in my own romantic fantasies. I invited my friends, photographers that I've worked with throughout my career, to create their own romantic images of me.

Seductive fantasy.

Inspired by Amadeus.

My seventeenth-century fantasy.

"Statue of Liberty" on a fifteenth-century wall.

Dressed as a Grecian maiden.

Dressed as Ophelia, daydreaming in our park.

7

Holding the Dream: Romantic Marriage

IT should only be in romantic novels that marriage marks the end of romance: marriage should be the beginning of a richer, deeper romance based on shared moments, shared memories, shared family: on listening, flirting, paying attention to his feelings as well as his words. Don't behave like a wife, behave like a mistress.

Nevertheless, a wedding should be something special. Find some way to make the wedding service your own. Perhaps include a favorite poem, or a piece of prose, and certainly choose your favorite hymns. Make it mean something to both of you. Perhaps you could borrow from another culture. After Greek Orthodox marriages they dance in the street, and Yugoslavian weddings include stealing the bride's shoes and auctioning them. The money goes to the newly wedded couple. Or you could do what friends of ours did: they let off thousands of helium balloons at the end of their wedding service, as an offering to the sky.

As I said earlier, my second husband, Geep, and I decided to get married on the spur of the moment. We had no money for wedding clothes but we wanted it to be special. I was filming *The Four Feathers* at the time, and the costumes were magnificent. Wouldn't it be wonderful, I thought, to be married in full Edwardian regalia—both of us and all our wedding party? The film company kindly agreed and lent us the costumes for our special day.

Then we were faced with the problem of where to celebrate after the ceremony. Again, we couldn't really afford a traditional, formal reception, so, because it was summer, we decided to have it out in the street. It happened to be the Queen's Silver Jubilee and everyone was having street parties, so we had our excuse. We invited everyone on the street and asked them all to bring food; they invited friends, who also brought food; all of our friends and family brought food—and presto! we had a small festival on our hands.

In the meantime, in true English fashion, it rained steadily for two weeks before the wedding, giving no sign of letting up. Not only was the wedding feast to be held outside, but we had arranged for an open carriage (another of the film's props) to bring us from the church to the reception. I suppose all brides are lucky, however, because on the day of the wedding, the rain stopped and the sun came out for twelve hours—just enough time to celebrate. I remem-

My wedding gown Edwardian style, given to me by the film costumiers Bermans.

ber that after the sun went in, it rained for two more weeks without a break.

My wedding to David was planned to be a dream wedding, perfect in every way.

Our friends John and Laurie Barry gave us our wedding at their house on Long Island, midway between our friends and family in Los Angeles and in England. We rented a gazebo, which was put on their estate. There were lawns down to the bay and a string quartet.

People arrived in seaplanes, in helicopters, in limos. We had to delay the wedding because of the traffic on the Long Island Expressway. By the time we were married, everyone was very merry. I passed out as they were taking the formal photos. By the end of the wedding, we had missed the last seaplane, and the limousine that was to take us back into town had broken down and was being repaired.

I found David and his friend John Barry sitting by the bay finishing off a bottle of Courvoisier, oblivious to everything. And I have to admit that that moment, seeing them sitting by the bay, was the best of all. They were so peaceful. The excitement and confusion, and now the peace, of that imperfect wedding was far more romantic than smoother occasions, where the perfection is dull. Romance is not perfection. It is life: dangerous, eventful, mysterious, and unpredictable life.

By the time we reached the Hotel Pierre in New York, where we were staying the night in honor of our reunion there a year or so before, we had both sobered up.

We were laughing as we walked into the room. But I was silenced when I saw the incredible midnight feast

Married at last, Gatsby-style, at John Barry's estate on Long Island.

David had arranged, with all our favorite luxurious, exotic foods, from oysters to lobsters.

It immediately brought back the memory of that night when Joe Jackson played in Central Park.

I turned to him. Our marriage had begun.

It was a thoughtful, imaginative idea, the kind of thinking that I suppose is expected on a marriage night. But don't end the romance there, on the marriage night. It's the beginning of the greatest romantic adventure of your life. On anniversaries, re-create something memorable from the wedding. One friend, who loves flowers, had especially fabulous flowers for her wedding. One anniversary her husband arranged for a florist to re-create one of the most beautiful of the bouquets to surprise his wife. You could prepare some of the same foods that were eaten at the reception, or you could reproduce the cake, or you could wear your wedding dress.

Every now and again David or I arrange a surprise night away with each other—on anniversaries it's the Hotel Pierre, for memory's sake. But we prepare other adventures for each other—surprise presents, surprise parties, surprise holidays. We try to keep our marriage alive, eventful, as romantic as it was the day of our wedding.

David has always had a flair for romance. He claims I'm so romantic he'd never have won me otherwise. But there's more to it than that. Only a real romantic would behave as David did on the opening night of *Amadeus*. I was upset because flowers and telegrams had arrived from everyone but him. At the last moment three dozen red roses were strewn across the room by

Katie as bridesmaid.

David and I in love at the beach before the wedding.

a mystery person—it was him. That was two minutes before the curtain rose and I had difficulty climbing over the sea of flowers.

Because David has been married before, he knows how easily marriages can fall apart if both partners don't try hard enough, don't treat marriage as a love affair. Who was it who said that twenty years of affairs turn a woman into a ruin, and twenty years of marriage into a public monument? Whoever it was, I shall add that if you combine the two—treat marriage as an affair—neither fate will be waiting for you. After twenty years you will still be a beautiful woman.

Of course, it's not always easy to keep a partnership as a love affair if you don't have help and you have children banging on your doors who want to crawl in bed with you in the morning and wake you up all night long. The point is, you must make time for each other. That is a priority. However little money is available, you can find a way round the problem. Make sure you leave the children with a friend sometimes, so you have the house to yourselves. Make sure you go out to dinner together. Make sure you take those weekends away. It doesn't have to be a weekend at the best hotel in town. Find somewhere pretty, and have a meal served up in the bedroom, with some chilled wine. Behave like the wicked, adulterous couple people will no doubt think you are.

In a new place you can discover each other again undistracted by the ironing, the telephone, all the things that wear you down. You can concentrate on each other. Make the time to talk, and to hold hands. Don't let your marriage drift: take hold of it and guide it.

Even if it's just one night away, just a few times a year, the children won't suffer if they're left with relatives or friends. They'll probably love it. As children, we always had plenty of friends stay with us when their parents were away, and we all loved it. Sometimes there would be as many as twelve children staying the night, crammed three to a bed. I can remember one midnight feast that included a hockey match and pop music at 3:00 A.M. The neighbors were not pleased. So don't worry too much when you leave your children occasionally. They'll probably love it as much as you will. Even if they're very young, a separation won't do them any harm.

Women often fall completely and romantically in love with their children. But it is important to make sure that you don't fall out of love with your partner, and he with you. So don't feel selfish when you leave your children. It is your happy marriage that will give them strength and security. That is far more important than being with them all the time. It is my loving family—my dear sisters and father and mother—who have given me the strength to be what I am. I know that whatever I do they will be there, loving me, loving each other, providing the fabric over which I can embroider my own life. Give your children that strength: make your marriage work. Put your husband first, for your children's sake as well as your own.

The greatest gift anyone can have is a happy relationship. Whatever disasters strike you, if your relationship is happy you can cope. It is worth working at. It is worth more than any number of dollars in a bank, any amount of success at work. Two people, sharing everything, in love, year after year, spending their lives together, supporting each other, encouraging each other.

I know that. My parents have a happy marriage. Though they're in their seventies, they still hold hands, watch sunsets, look after each other as they travel adventurously together all over the world—Malaysia one week, Los Angeles the next. He is the intellectual, she is the organizer. They make a great pair. My mother's love for my father and my father's for my mother have given my sisters and me great support and inspiration. He treasures her and looks after her, and she does the same for him.

I don't blame people who have affairs outside their marriage. But affairs are not an easy option. They can tear you apart and leave you with nothing. In every relationship you have to examine what is constructive and what is destructive. There is so much about affairs that can be destructive. What is constructive and exciting is, of course, the mystery and the romance of having only a short time together. I try to bring those elements into my marriage—the elements of change, excitement, drama, and having to pack so much into a short time. I'm sharing my husband with his business and he's sharing me with mine. There's no boredom. Think of your work as your marriage and your marriage as your affair—make the most of what you have, think positively, think creatively, keep your love alive.

Don't sit around complaining that life is dreary, your marriage is dreary. Neither is. You are the one who is dreary if you think that life is dull. Life isn't, so long as you look up and around, and see and share the magic and wonder in you, in your loved ones, in the trees and the flowers, and everything all around you.

If, like so many women, you are married to a confirmed nonromantic, ask him to read this book for his own sake. What I'm talking about is how to have a happy life, and who doesn't want that? There's nothing undignified about trying to live enjoyably, with a certain respect for ecstasy and exuberance. They should try it. Half the men in America are too exhausted from working hard in order to enjoy themselves at some future date to enjoy themselves at all. By the time they finally decide they've made it, they've forgotten how to enjoy themselves. And women are doing this, too. Now that there is often no one at home keeping the up quality of life, making sure that there are flowers on the table, bread in the breadbox, a clean tablecloth ready, it is even more important that men and women think about romance and living in a way that is romantic. Life is precious, and very short. Men and women who work should make sure they don't throw away all that is precious in their desire to achieve and to keep busy. It is important also to learn how not to be busy, to learn to stand still.

The work ethic is fine. There's nothing wrong with that. The great English Romantics of the nineteenth century were all hard workers. If you want to live a marvelous, joyful life you have to work at it harder than those who make do with something mediocre. Nothing comes ready-made. If your partner is a workaholic ask him what it's all for, and ask yourself. Make sure you find the time to enjoy the world you've been born into. Remember: you have all the time there is. It isn't enough to take a walk every so often. You have to use your eyes, and your ears, and all your senses. You have to look in order to see. That butterfly or that bird

Using flowers for the Pre-Raphaelite look.

The wedding, with the flowers finally in my hair.

is better than any fabric your hard-earned money can buy.

Make sure you enjoy the gifts that are free. Don't spend all your time striving for the things that aren't free, and spoiling your marriage through overwork in the process.

It is our world. That is what some of us forget. We are all just a part of nature—the bare pattern of a tree mirrors the pattern of our veins—so we should enjoy nature and be at ease with it instead of hustling and bustling our way through it. A few minutes of peace the two of you spend together by the sea or in the woods will help your marriage, help you to be at ease with each other.

Look together in the same direction. Look properly. Enjoy life together. We are so used to being spoon-fed films and television programs that sometimes we don't bother to look around us, and it does require a certain concentration to look at the beauty all about—the perfection of a rose, the shape of a cloud, the smell of the air just before it rains. It is necessary to pause for a little while and be still and together allow yourselves to see and to feel.

Together run through the sand, walk through piles of leaves, hold hands, kiss in a park like young lovers, wander by rivers at night hand in hand.

The rule that runs through all of life is that nothing can be static: politics, relationships, nature. Once something ceases to grow, it is dying. In order for a relationship to stay alive, it cannot stay as it is; it has to change, to develop.

Support each other. David cannot cope well with death, and recently two couples we know lost children in their twenties. I can help by talking him through grief, and did in these cases. When such terrible things happen, David and I are reminded of how much the quality of life matters, sharing life and enjoying life rather than just acquiring and achieving.

Talk to each other about things that matter, about what you both want out of life. Never leave your marriage to look after itself. It needs looking after, feeding, or it will die.

If you appreciate your world, you will communicate your joy to your partner. Together walk through the park in the early morning, or when the first snow has fallen. Don't shiver and stay inside, in the trap of your own conformity. Live a little.

Because trees don't run multimillion-dollar advertising campaigns extolling their merits, and flowers are only advertised when arranged in bunches in shops, let us not become so dazed by our money-orientated culture that we lose sight of the most precious gifts each person alive has, gifts that are presented free, at birth, on arrival on this planet. No big business offers such excellent free gifts as the snow and the wind and the sun and the leaves that toss on the trees and fall gently on the ground providing piles for you to walk through like a child.

Enjoy it all together. Don't treat life as a struggle. It's an adventure—but you have to seek out the adventures together.

*　*　*

Occasionally do something wildly, ridiculously romantic. Kidnap your husband, for instance. Just arrange a secret holiday for him and make sure he suspects nothing. Check with his colleagues to make sure that it is all right for him to take a certain week or few days off. Organize everything perfectly. Organization lies at the heart of a busy, romantic life if it is to be a success.

On that Monday morning, when he is dressing for work, tell him to dress more casually, but don't tell him why. He might protest a little at first—but if you plan properly, all will be well.

I took David off to Mexico on a kidnap holiday after two weeks of clandestine organization with travel agents, his colleagues at work, with nannies and secretaries.

At first he was appalled. "But I've got appointments. . . ."

"They've been canceled."

"But my colleagues . . . I can't leave them with all the work."

"Don't worry. They knew you were going two weeks ago. It's all organized."

"But . . ."

"Come on."

A call to his secretary put him at ease and once he knew everything really had been taken care of, he sat back and relaxed.

I had booked an expensive room in the hotel, but when we arrived there we discovered a much more romantic room, on the beach. We could hear the sea from it.

"To hell with the expense," said David. "Let's have it."

We asked if the room was available, and it was. To our astonishment it was much cheaper than our original room. What puzzled us, however, was the Mexicans' surprise that we should want the lovely beach room.

All went well. David felt he had been transported into another world. He is so used to being the organizer that it was marvelous for him to know he could relax and be looked after.

However, the following morning we very nearly were literally transported into another world. We woke to find the room—our clothes, the furniture, and very nearly us—under a few feet of water.

No wonder the Mexicans were surprised we wanted that room.

We decided the next day to go for a romantic horseback ride. Wearing my tiniest tank top, which has narrow straps (the kind that sexily drops off the shoulders from time to time), and a pair of blue jeans, I rode off with David into the sunset. Our guide, a Mexican boy of ten who spoke no English, put me on a pregnant horse—supposedly made tamer by her condition. The horses took off at a gallop. My tank top kept slipping, and in my determination to stay alive I gave up on it and galloped naked to the waist. Our guide, seeing this, decided his services were no longer necessary and disappeared, leaving us riding into the sunset until we finally arrived at a beach with a beautiful deserted lighthouse. This was romantic—scary but romantic.

If things had gone too smoothly that holiday wouldn't have been nearly so memorable. Romance is adventure. It's the things that go wrong, that are unexpected. It's not the bland lovely face of a girl; it's the face of a girl with mystery, with a sense of adventure, with a sense that contact with her could make everything go very wrong indeed, or very right. Dangerous men are romantic too, as many women have found to their cost. A beaming, good-natured, respectable man might make a good husband in some ways, but unless you bring out the danger in him, he'll make a boring lover, and really good husbands should be lovers too. If you oppress him with your strength, you'll turn him into merely a good-natured companion. Show him your femininity as well as your strength, so that he will show you his masculinity as well as his kindness.

Who wants to make love to someone night after night who is just a good chum? Your imagination can turn him into whomever you like, of course, but imagination can go only so far alone. It needs to be rooted in some reality.

Make sure you frequently arrange holidays or weekends away, or even evenings, in which you can play those old roles of lover and his lass.

When you're having your romantic trysts, don't discuss the mortgage or the problem of the leaking roof: listen to each other, flatter each other with your interest in each other, pretend you've known each other a week instead of years. There is no doubt that there is nothing quite like young love. Make sure you keep some freshness, some sense of discovery. As your love grows older, keep it young.

Do you remember your first love? I'll never forget mine. He is now one of Britain's top astronomers, James Emerson. But in those days he was just the boy next door. We used to swap stamps. If he accidentally wrote "Love from Jimmy" on the bottom of a gift, I would tear out that little piece of paper and carry it around everywhere close to my heart, because it had the word "love" on it. That's when I realized I was a confirmed romantic.

I am equally romantic about David. I keep all his letters, treasure everything he has ever given me, from flowers I keep pressed to the beautiful shawl he bought me when he first knew I was pregnant. I value that because it was such a thoughtful, carefully chosen present, but mostly because it was from him.

Marriage is a beginning, not an end. I read recently of a couple who revived their earlier feelings of romance by making love in their car parked in their drive. That seems a little excessive. But certainly love should never be respectably formal; it should always be a little dangerous, a little wicked, and all too often marriage can take that wickedness away.

Don't be too respectably married. Keep an element of mystery, of unpredictability, of danger between you both. I often think of Charlie, my second real boyfriend, who was a wild, handsome young man. He used secretly to serenade my room from the garden below with the help of a walkie-talkie as I lay in bed at night (my mother was firm about bedtime because I had to get up so early to travel to ballet school). One day, instead of a bunch of flowers, he uprooted one of my mother's plants, complete with worms, and threw it up into my bedroom window!

That wasn't romantic, but it was certainly unpredictable! And it is vital to keep an element of unpredictability in a relationship.

One very romantic woman treats her marriage like one long romance. On her husband's last birthday she organized a complete secret day for him, starting with breakfast at the London hotel, Brown's, then a test drive around Hyde Park Corner in the Mercedes he'd always wanted to drive, then a video in bed of John Lennon's "Imagine," then the afternoon in bed, then a surprise party for him with all his closest friends. Everything was unexpected, surprising. Take the trouble to give pleasure to your lover. Take trouble over his life, over your life. Share new adventures, new places. Don't allow love to grow dim and overfamiliar. You are a new person every day. Don't forget that. Grow together—don't grow apart.

When I was young I used to envy the rich talking and laughing in lighted restaurants while I was walking by outside, looking in. But now that I'm one of the people in the lighted restaurants, sometimes I envy those outside, the people still struggling, because struggle is romantic.

Of course, people do inevitably change within a marriage, and some marriages will simply never work, however hard you both try. But respect marriage. Try to change together. Do all you can to keep your marriage safe and strong. It can bring you more happiness than anything else in the world. And divorce is a very, very painful experience.

8

Juggling Romance and The Busy Life

Most women have many roles to play: worker, mother, wife, hostess. And now, as if you're not exhausted enough by all these, here I come adding to the list and asking you to be romantic too. But without this romantic quality all the other roles are just a list. It is this quality that makes sense of them all. In the search for success we shouldn't lose happiness, a flair for living, a delight in our surroundings, in each other. What is the point of trying to become a superwoman if in the process we lose our souls?

If you try to do too much—to juggle too many things at once—there is always the danger that you will drop the lot. But I prefer to live dangerously. It keeps me excited about life, and there is nothing less romantic

Romance and the busy life—on the set of Lassiter *with Katie.*

than someone who is bored.

Even the disasters are funny, in retrospect. I used to take my first child, Katie, on location with me, and my husband would come to wherever we were every ten days to two weeks, stay for a long weekend, then dash back. It was hectic. The first film I did was when Katie was three months old. I decided I was going to be Supermom. I had had to stop breast-feeding because of the film, and our pediatrician told me Katie must have a particular brand of soy formula milk. The special tins were, so I thought, brilliantly organized in strong trunks for the plane flight.

At the Los Angeles airport the baggage collapsed— the trunks just fell open, spilling tons of diapers and formula tins all over everywhere. I had to ditch them all, grab the baby and the new nanny, whom I'd known for only two days, and catch the flight for Hungary, where I was filming. In Hungary they had none of the necessities I'd left behind. They had wonderful goulash, but you can't feed a three-month-old baby goulash.

You can't aim for the skies—try to do everything— and not occasionally fail. Failure doesn't matter. It's trying that matters. A true romantic can overcome any disaster because a true romantic knows that there is always the next time.

For me romance is part of my work, part of my life, and it's something I want to pass on to my children. I don't want to be just a juggler, any more than you do. I want to have a certain beauty in my life, to have a sense of the past as well as to have hopes for the future.

My priorities have always been: my husband, my children, and then my work. We decided that a long

My parents—the ultimate romantics!

Presenting my first Oscar.

time ago. I saw friends of mine who were happily married and then had children but were so obsessed with the children that they completely forgot their husbands and ended up divorced and wondering what single parenting was all about. For the sake of the children, apart from any other considerations, I believe a husband should come first. What greater gift can you give to a child than a happy and stable family background? It might seem to be best for them if you spend all your time and attention on them rather than on your husband, but in the long run it's unkind if it jeopardizes your marriage.

I want my children to have what I had, a marvelous childhood and two parents who love each other. Mine stood solidly together. There was no point in us telling tales about one parent to the other. We knew that Mummy and Daddy were one. We had to stand by their decisions. It worked very well. We are still a close family, very warm, very caring for each other. Their close, romantic relationship gave all three of us—Joyce, Sally, and Anne—a great sense of security. That security has given all three of us a sense of freedom and romance.

David is a very successful man in our industry on the other side from mine, the business side. He's one of the people nobody hears about, who makes deals and tries to get the children of clients out of jail when they're in trouble, and manages the taxes. His work goes on day and night. He gets calls at three in the morning. They're never for me. I go to executive functions as his wife. I'm not a full-time wife and therefore I often feel I'm not as good as the rest of them, but I'm trying, I'm learning.

The other side of my life with David is when he's my husband and the photographers shove him out of the way so they can take photographs of me and my latest leading man, as if David doesn't exist. Fortunately, he is a very understanding husband.

He's a good juggler too. Often he wakes early, at 4:00 A.M., because he has things on his mind. But he makes his sleeplessness into something positive. He makes lists of the things that are on his mind, or he looks after one of the babies, or, if I'm away, he'll put on a video of one of my films and watch it if he misses me.

Lists are a great help for the workaholic. If you have to go to business lunches and you are frustrated by the wasted half hours spent getting there and back, waiting at traffic lights, being stuck in traffic, instead of fretting, be constructive. Before leaving for lunch take some notes or proposals with you or just make lists. Working can help release anxieties, because you're busy and helping to get one more thing done. It's a good idea to use lost time—time spent in cars, in planes, time that would otherwise be spent worrying and waiting. Use it to write letters, for instance, to express your worries and frustrations or to express your love for someone. The time you gain by doing tasks and saving yourself worry can give you time to do something pleasurable—sit in a park, watch children playing, buy some flowers.

Life and time are all you have—use them well.

As I say, David is my top priority. Next, after my husband, come my children.

At 5:30 our daughter, Katie, comes into bed with us, and we have an hour together, to play, cuddle, and talk. At 6:30 she gets ready to go to school and goes off five days a week in the school bus. The pediatrician said she's not supposed to climb into bed with me in the morning, but it's one of the few times I get to talk to her. The nanny dresses her for school, and I stay in bed with David. We spend the time doing the usual things husbands and wives do in bed, and we talk—about big business, about life in general. We make sure we have time for each other.

Of course I am sad about not always having the time to choose what Katie will wear each day, and because someone else sometimes gives her her bath and breakfast. But she is a very happy child, and it is more important for her and for our marriage that David and I have some real time together before the phones start ringing and business takes over.

Nobody calls me for business when he's in the house, because it's our home, the place we come to relax, even though it's my office during the day. I have a secretary in the house and two lines that ring constantly, but I try to tell everyone not to call before 9:30 in the morning. Otherwise, the house isn't our home, it's an extension of our business lives.

You have to respect each other, to think about each other, to make concessions. When I was younger I wasn't ready for that—I was too full of the selfishness of youth. Now I'm ready. It is necessary to plan your life with your partner and children well. It's no good assuming everything will be fine. Use your intelligence, your imagination, your inventiveness to make it fine. Be sure to listen, and make time for each other. But also make sure you spend time and listen to your children. Keep the right balance, for you and for them.

I remember when I was pregnant with Sean that I

Pregnant—wondering who this will be and starting to write this book.

After my baby shower for Sean.

would lie in bed with the baby moving inside me, and I would think: Who is this? This is great. This is exciting. I don't know how it's all going to work out. It's more exciting than anything.

People say, "I'd love to be an actress. How glamorous!" But nothing ever comes close to having children: nothing. Even though I can't give up everything else to have children, and I need my work, children are much more important.

Sometimes, of course, I feel I've failed, and I end up in a corner in tears, devastated because I'm not with my children enough, but what holds me together is what my mother taught me. I feel I can only do my best.

My children have been enormously tolerant of my work. Children accept the concept of the father going out to work and coming home. They develop wonderful relationships with their fathers. There is no reason why they shouldn't do the same with their mothers. You don't have to be a full-time mother. If you have other interests, there is nothing wrong with pursuing them. Indeed, the child is far better off with a busy, fulfilled mother and a good nanny than a miserable, frustrated mother who does not enjoy staying at home. Besides, as they grow up they will be proud of your achievements, proud of your identity. Even now Katie loves to see me dress up for fashion spreads, although she is puzzled by my love scenes in films.

"That isn't Daddy," she'll say, looking at me accusingly.

"It's only pretend," I say.

Everyone has an opinion on what you should and shouldn't do with your children. Some say to me that I shouldn't let my children be photographed, because they might get kidnapped. But I can't see myself going through airports throwing a coat over Katie's face every time we go past a paparazzo. What would the child think?

When Katie was three months old, *Vogue* wanted to photograph us together, to run eleven pages on us . . . I couldn't resist it. How could I tell my daughter when she was twenty-one and beautiful that I had turned down the chance of photographs in *Vogue*?

She's turned out to be amazingly resilient to my career. It's no big deal to her. She thinks that it's normal to have a mother on television and on magazine covers. She accepts my going off to premieres with diamonds all over me, looking like a Hollywood movie star one moment and the next dealing with car pools. She thinks nothing of it. I remember my father, a surgeon, coming home for lunch spattered with blood, and that was perfectly normal to me. I never queried what he did. I used to laugh at the jokes about gynecologists, but I had no idea what the word meant.

I knew I was proud of my father, though. My parents remind me that at school I used to tell the girls, "You're not supposed to do this. I'm a doctor's daughter and I know." When I returned home I would say, "They wouldn't listen to me. And I *told* them I was a doctor's daughter." They gave me an honorary degree, Joyce Frankenberg, D.D. (Doctor's Daughter).

Of course, I do get tired, especially with a baby to look after too. I change diapers and get up at night for Sean. I think, Oh, I don't want to get up and do this; maybe he'll be quiet. . . . But those moments you spend, those moments of communication at 3:00 A.M.

Enjoying Katie.

Enjoying Sean in Hawaii.

when everything is quiet, and there is just you and the baby looking up at you with sweet eyes: they are beautiful. You forget who you are and where you are . . . there's just you and the baby. I need these moments in a very complicated life.

When you work hard you need some peace. But perhaps even more than that you need a sense of humor. That is perhaps the greatest help when things go wrong, as they do in busy lives. It was something I learned from Roger Moore. He said: "If you laugh at yourself and send yourself up first, then other people can't do it to you. If you can find the humor in something you do not find humorous in yourself at all, then you'll survive."

In my profession, you need to.

Every now and then I pinch myself when I suddenly realize that very famous people do come up to me and say, "Hi, Jane. I really enjoyed your last film." I'm always totally mortified and embarrassed that they know who I am and have seen what I've done. It's exciting when it's somebody you really respect, someone like Jane Fonda, Shirley MacLaine, women who are much more than just actresses, who have led rounded lives. It wouldn't be difficult to let it all go to one's head. It is vital to maintain a sense of humor and constantly to be aware of one's faults and limitations as well as one's achievements.

There are problems specific to every career. Separation is one David and I have to cope with. It is important to find out how long you can be apart before it all cracks up. For us, it's about ten days. After ten days, one of us has to get on an airplane. We know this. We work it into our schedule if we possibly can.

Taking a nap in a hammock with Katie for the Vogue *shoot.*

The other essential is to communicate as much as you can while you're apart, so that although you're separated in distance you're together in spirit.

We talk almost every day when I'm filming. He tells me what is happening in his life, and I tell him what I am doing, so that each shares the life of the other.

We know we need this kind of contact. A successful partnership must be built on self-knowledge. It's no good planning a business trip that takes a month if you crack up after a week. It sounds obvious but it is surprising how many people ignore the facts about themselves. It's one thing to be mysterious to other people, quite another to be mysterious to yourself.

I often turn down work because geographically it is impossible, or else I ask the producers if it's possible to film it near to home. A recent film, *Obsessed with a Married Woman*, seems to take place in New York, but I only did the film on condition it was shot in Los Angeles. Only two days were shot in New York, and the scenes in Connecticut were really shot in Malibu.

But however hard I try, there are times when I have to be away from my family. My children have had to deal with a certain amount of separation right from the start. Mine have adapted well to it: you can adapt a child to change. I don't create a routine for them which, if broken, would be devastating for them.

One day I went to a parent-teacher meeting and heard a parent say: "My son isn't yet capable of being away from me for an extra hour a day." I was grateful that my children have been able to accept my absence. I believe it is because they feel secure. The bond of breast-feeding is very important: it helps you and the baby grow to love one another. The quality of the time you spend together matters too. It mustn't be time when you shove them in front of the television and carry on with the ironing or whatever else you have to do. It's when you stop everything and spend time with the child talking about things *the child* wants to talk about, rather than things you want to talk about. Or you watch a movie again and again with them, even if you are bored to tears. I am currently watching *The Secret of Nimh* every night. I've somehow or other given Katie the knowledge that Mummy's always there is she needs me. Perhaps it comes from taking her around the world with me while I was working. Even if I were working a fourteen-hour day, at least I would see her in the morning and at night.

Now that she's at school, she can't travel with me, which is sad, and sometimes I am lonely.

People ask me how I have the energy to do all that I do. The energy comes from romantic thinking and good juggling and an ability to be like a child. When you think romantically you are curious and open to change, yet you concentrate hard on each thing as it comes up. It's the way to achieve a full and vigorous life. It's the way to change your life—to be happy.

When I'm away I often buy Katie presents to make me feel close to her. Sometimes I see her looking really uncomfortable in some dress or sweater.

"I hate it," she tells the nanny, "but I'm wearing it because Mummy bought it."

She loves going on shopping trips with me, especially to buy shoes. Recently I went out to lunch with one of my best friends, whose child was born twenty minutes after mine in the same hospital. We took our four-year-olds to a very chic Beverly Hills restaurant and let our girls dress up for their first ladies luncheon.

At the end of the meal Katie said, very formally, "I've enjoyed that—now can we take you somewhere next time?"

"Yes," we said, "that would be lovely. Where?"

"Chuck-e-Cheese"—a pizza place somewhat like a cross between an amusement arcade and Disneyland. My idea of hell—but we had fun there too.

9

Starting Early: Giving Your Children A Sense of the Romantic

Iᴛ was Bertrand Russell who wrote, "To kill fancy in childhood is to make a slave to what exists, a creature tethered to earth and therefore unable to create heaven."

As a parent, I believe one's greatest duty is to bring up a child who can create heaven on earth, someone who has the imagination and hope to be happy.

That is what my parents gave me—imagination and hope.

Our washing line, hung with sheets, used to be the curtain behind which we would prepare our shows. A raised area in the attic was another "stage." We had a dressing-up box full of funny old hats and dresses. My mother used to collect bits and pieces from garage

Katie, dressed up, trying Mummy's job and taking it very seriously.

Dressing up for fun—Katie playing the Fairy Princess, Jenni the Geisha.

sales and charity jumble sales for the box, because she remembered one from her own childhood, at a country house she used to visit. I can still remember the heaven of plunging my hand into that seemingly bottomless trunk full of necklaces, hats, velvets, and satins. Now Katie has one too, so she can turn herself into a Spanish lady one day, a Hawaiian girl the next.

My parents took us to museums, to art galleries, to ballets, and to the theater. They showed us the world and its wonders. When we were very young they took us to the immense opera house at Covent Garden, all three girls dressed in red velvet cloaks with silk lining. My parents were, I think, inspired by the romantic looks of their three girls, with our long hair and pretty faces, all close to the same age, like the Brontës, like the Little Women, like Chekhov's Three Sisters, like Botticelli's Three Graces. Our looks and our ages and the unconventional nature of our parents set us all a little apart, in a world of our own, of plays and dances and dreams. With them, no one day was like another. We never knew what to expect. Skating one day, the theater the next, ten people to dinner, fifteen to stay the night. We are still all a little like that. Anne follows her dream of a happy family life, Sally hers of travel and adventure. They are both as unconventional as they've always been; exceptional, entertaining, beautiful girls. Sally played my double in the film *Dark Mirror* but disliked the world of acting and was happy to return to her life of travel, turning up anywhere in the world at a moment's notice.

I used to feel, as I sat in the theater in Covent Garden, that I belonged up there on the stage, with the music and the movement and the color and the beauty.

135

Katie and Jenni in flamenco dresses I found in Spain while shooting The Sun Also Rises.

Sean, dressed up for dinner in a hotel room, on location in Frankfurt for War and Remembrance.

My parents sent these dreams spinning through my head.

If I go to ballets nowadays, I watch the faces of little girls: they're wide-eyed, full of amazement, entranced. And then I look back at the ballerinas and I still see what I used to see: that other, fairy-tale world out there on the stage. That is the world my parents showed us— and I wish to show my children. I want to instill in my children zest, hope, wonderment.

My parents involved us in their lives. We used to go to the hospital with my father when we were very young, and be given special nursing outfits and particular tasks to do, such as making cotton swabs out of mounds of cotton wool. We were always introduced to guests, taught to converse properly with them, altogether brought up as important people in the household rather than nuisances to be hidden away when grownups arrived. I think this respect our parents gave us built up in us a self-respect which is a great help in difficult times.

My parents gave me the strength to be romantic, to follow my dreams, because they made me know they would always be there, even if I failed, loving me, encouraging me. And I know I still have that safety net. Whatever happens, they'll be there.

I want my children to know the same feeling. I want them to have the courage to try, and to pick themselves up if they fail. A warm, loving, secure background matters more than anything for a child. The family should be the base that frees them, the security that allows a child to be strong and free. Make sure your children grow up with a proper sense of security and wonderment, so that they can become romantic adults who

RIGHT: *A charity fashion show for the Emanuels with Katie and Jenni.*

BELOW: *Acting out a scary story for Jenni.*

have innocence and adaptability.

The moment your child is born, relish its independence. The child isn't you or your husband. He or she is another person, someone you're going to live with. Allow him or her to be an individual.

And don't push your children too hard. Don't turn them into overachieving, stressed children without a proper sense of youth and creativity. Give them something to look back on. Don't just give them memories of desks and paperwork.

Friends of ours found a little chest, bashed it up so that it looked old, and filled it with rock crystals and cheap and cheerful bits of glitz and junk jewelry. Then, when they were on holiday, they wrote to the children that they had found a Treasure Chest sticking out of the sand. They brought the box home, and the little girls were over the moon about it.

The father then said: "You know, I was looking through some old books in our house . . . and look what I found . . . it seems to be a map." Their mother had burned the edges of a piece of paper so that it looked old. She had written on it a guide that said there was treasure actually buried in their house.

The father took the children down into the cellar of the house, and there, in an old sherry bottle filled by the mother with play money, trinkets, rocks, and mother-of-pearl shells, was the treasure. The little girls were thrilled.

That's a lovely, secret, romantic thing to do for a child at an early age.

The same friend said that when his son was two years old, they went for a walk, and he explained that the son should pick a flower for his mother. So the boy

Cooking with Katie in Los Angeles.

The Easter rabbits! The large one is my father.

picked the flower he wanted and presented it to his mother, who put it in a special vase. If you start children young with that kind of gesture, it's something that stays with them forever and ever.

A good party also helps to bring out a child's imagination. Mine always have a theme of some sort. The last one turned everyone into Easter rabbits, and my father became the Easter Bunny. The children went into my bathroom, and I smeared clown white on their faces and painted on red noses and whiskers; they all became rabbits and had great fun. When the parents came to pick them up and saw the children in the pool with gray-white faces, they thought they had been freezing to death for four hours.

Our first children's party was "Wild Things and Fairies," based on a book by Maurice Sendak. Each child turned up as a wild thing or a fairy. They loved it. The disguises freed them, filled them with excitement.

Another party turned into a game. I hadn't ordered a big party cake, so I rushed off to Safeway to buy some small plain ones, and decorating them became the central party game. Five children decorated them, using icing from tubes, M&Ms, raisins, and hundreds and thousands of sprinkles.

Why not have making the cake be part of the party? Ask the children to help make the cake, then organize plenty of games. When they return, the cake will be ready to eat. You can also do this with large cookies.

Encourage the children to make their own hats by providing basic party hats and brightly colored stickers, or else provide pieces of gold and silver cardboard that they can cut up and glue together to make crowns. Buy a cheap sun dress and let your child decorate it with stickers. I did this for Katie's birthday and she loved it.

The best time of all for children, in America especially, is Halloween, when they all dress up and act out their fantasies. I feared I might not have brought up a romantic child when I asked Katie what she would like to dress up as one Halloween. I said she could be anything in the world and assumed she'd want to be a princess. But she wanted to be a shark!

Help your child to be creative and uninhibited, to appreciate the beauty in the world. Make time to read to your children, to invent games with them, to go for walks, guide them toward some understanding of the marvels of the world and their own minds.

Most people stumble through life using only a tiny segment of their minds. Let your children be different. Free their minds. But always, behind the freedom, provide the security. Let them know that the world is a safe place because you are there.

10

Dressing the Part: Accessorizing The Romantic Life

WHEN, as a little girl, I was taken on a birthday treat to the opera at Covent Garden to see our family friend Amy Shuard performing as Aïda, we went backstage afterward. I saw her pull off her eyelashes, take off her wig, lipstick. Under all that make-up and costume was Auntie Amy. It was a mesmerizing transformation—from the princess who had suffocated in a tomb to my Auntie Amy.

On that day I decided to be a ballet dancer. I stood on the empty stage and knew I'd be on it one day, dressed up as someone else.

From that day, too, I loved all the arts that deal in transformations. Clothes are much more to me than merely the appropriate things to wear for different occasions. Instead, they are the magical garments I put on to transform myself into anyone I choose. Nor do I see make-up as just something to enhance the features. I see it as paint, and it should be used as paint: paint your face, change yourself, transform.

Playing different characters, in life or in work, is a way of finding out which is the real self. The characters I've created on film all have a little bit of me in them, and that is one reason I like to keep most of the clothes I've acted in. Collecting clothes is one of my passions. A long time ago, my great-aunt gave me her old forties clothes, and I wear them and treasure them. This was the beginning of my fascination with period clothes, of which I now have a formidable collection. My closets are full of the women I have been—Lady Brett Ashley's flapper costumes from *The Sun Also Rises,* Edwardian straw hats from *Somewhere in Time,* casual California-girl looks from *Haunting Passion,* leopardskin and leather from *Dark Mirror,* classic forties clothes from my part as the vamp Hilary in *Crossings.* All these different characters are in my wardrobes. I love dressing up, creating other characters in photographs as well as on film.

I can still, in my mind's eye, see Auntie Amy's costume hanging up on the hook in her dressing room, the costume which had but a short while before held the dramatic princess Aïda.

Anyone can play at transformations. Wear a velvet dress and become Vivien Leigh in *Gone with the Wind.* If you've never worn red lipstick, wear it and become Rita Hayworth. If you want long hair, wear a hairpiece. Color your hair with the wash-out rinses and discover the excitement of being a redhead perhaps.

Forties dress given to me by my Great Aunt Becky.

I discovered my Rita Hayworth side while searching out the character of Hilary for Crossings.

Women have become too lacking in mystery. Now is the time for romance and its companion, mystery, to return to our lives. Try veils, hats, antique jewelry, lockets. Don't reveal too easily who is in the locket: just stare moodily into the distance and smile a tender, tragic smile. Life is for fun, danger, romance: live it. Don't take your clothes off hours after meeting some man: keep them on, plenty of them, keep him guessing, keep him entranced. Be the witch woman, the temptress, the outdoor girl. Don't bore him with your down-to-earth approach to sex and love. Don't bore yourself. I'm not suggesting that clothes shouldn't be sensual. They certainly should. What they shouldn't be is obvious.

Wear long evening dresses that bare your shoulders. A long dress immediately gives a woman a pleasant feeling of vulnerability. Even the hardest, most successful careerwomen gather up a little old-fashioned vulnerability when they gather up their skirts at a grand ball.

It takes me back in time, to a more leisured world where women were looked after by men. I don't want that world, of course I don't. Anyone who knows me will say that vulnerability is by no means my most obvious quality. I don't long to be pushed around by men, to be uneducated, to live in the past. But we should make sure we hold onto the valuable aspects of the past, in particular the respect for a woman's femininity, and for a man's masculinity. Don't let us all turn into standardized, asexual creatures.

Different ages have different styles, of course, and what suits one woman won't suit another. I have a small waist, so the age of crinolines with tiny waists and huge flouncy skirts suits me well. My wedding dress is a dress like that. I wear it in the advertisement for Le Jardin, the fragrance I help promote. They couldn't come up with anything nearly as romantic.

It is white with a blue sash, and was designed by a friend, Geoffrey Holder, as a wedding gift. A ballet costume company called Grace Costumes made the dress. Two wonderful Italian ladies worked on it day and night, and when I first saw it . . . I was overwhelmed. It is a really extraordinary fantasy dress.

It had pleats over my bosom and it just spread as far as the eye could see—hundreds of yards of silk organza. They had turned me into a fairy princess. Tears were in my eyes because they had made something so special. I simply could not believe how beautiful it was.

The ladies looked at me and said: "This is our gift to you."

I was completely overwhelmed.

Sometimes, on our wedding anniversary, I put on the dress for a surprise, and David and I have a wonderful dinner together.

For the wedding day I wanted my hair in my very own style, of no particular age. I wanted it to be like Ophelia's, wild and free and long and loose . . . but at the same time as if someone had thrown a mass of fresh flowers onto my hair and some had clung there.

So we made tiny, tiny braids in my hair—about twenty-five of them from top to bottom, so tiny you couldn't even see they were there, and we sewed fresh flowers into the braids.

They looked stunning until the flowers started dying, and when evening came I couldn't get the braids undone. I spent the first four hours after the wedding

Preparing for the wedding, braiding flowers into my hair.

trying to undo my braids. My husband and I were both working at it, as was every friend who remained. I was ready to cut the whole thing off. It is not a style that I recommend to anyone for their wedding night.

That was one romantic idea that didn't work out very well.

Romance is about being uninhibited and changing your image. People are so busy they don't think to do the unusual. We become so stuck in images and styles that we don't think to change, or perhaps we just don't have the courage to do something different. Either subtle or drastic changes can get you out of your rut and make you feel different and special.

If you always wear classic clothes, why not add an antique lace collar to your plain cardigan. It doesn't take much trouble, merely the lace collar and two safety pins.

And certainly every woman should try wearing sexy underwear. It immediately gives you a different sense of yourself. If you don't feel sexy before you put it on, you will afterward.

If you never take risks, take a risk. Do something daring—wear a slinky black dress. First of all, go to a department store and try one on. Why not? If you don't like it, it's done you no harm. Go to shops and try on different styles. Don't be embarrassed. Nobody knows you at the store. Why shouldn't you try on some outrageous clothes? But when you do go shopping, make sure you put on make-up and wear your favorite outfit, so that you only buy something better than what you have, not something awful that simply looks a bit less awful than what you have on.

I'd always thought that the twenties style of dress

Our men dressed for the New Year's Eve Black Tie or Better party. David center, my father to his left.

New Year's Eve with the family. I'm wearing my antique paste tiara.

wasn't for me: I preferred tight waists and full skirts. But while filming *The Sun Also Rises* I discovered that those low waistlines can make small and not terribly fit people look long and fit and very sexy. Try a low waistline, beads, and a ribbon around your hair, try different styles, different ages, and see in which age you feel most comfortable. Why settle for now when you could exist in any age just by a little dressing up?

Wear jewelry but don't feel you have to wear real jewelry. Fake jewels are just as good, no one ever knows the difference. I love fake diamond earrings.

Men can dress up too. Men look great in uniforms, and for our New Year's Eve parties in England the men rent uniforms, find them in junk or antique stores or wear their own or their fathers'. We collect these costumes, and have jackets and waistcoats from as far back as 1790.

I once read a book set in the future, when all conditions were perfect, we lived forever, we didn't need clothes or food, everything was redundant except for one thing. People wore glasses over their eyes, because when they took their glasses off, and their eyes communicated in the raw with another pair of eyes, it was their most intimate moment of love-making. That to me epitomizes the romantic look. It's a game of hide-and-seek. Men are different in uniforms. They hold themselves differently. They behave differently. They become a little more mysterious. With fans, veils, long dresses, women acquire a flirtatious, feminine manner. The quest and the chase are the most exciting part of romance. Courtship is a game that if played right can lead to a lifetime of happiness. But if it's managed clumsily, too quickly, if it lacks style and a respect for

Sunglasses—today's equivalent of last century's fan.

Veils can add such mystery to an antique hat.

the mystery of the other person, it can be meaningless and even depressing.

Men fall in love with women they don't quite know, women who seem to say, "There is something about me you haven't discovered yet, an angle, an aspect, a fantasy." Men seldom fall in love with the matter-of-fact.

Veils are especially suitable for romantics. Even just a little veiling over a hat. A veil provides that air of distance, of dreaminess, of perhaps some past grief. It intrigues.

Actresses are probably more skillful than most people at knowing how to provoke particular moods in people. After all, our job is to control the moods of our audiences. We have seen again and again how a little bright lipstick, or a little veiling, or a way of standing, can set the appropriate tone for a scene. Even as you read this you can probably imagine the beautiful woman sitting alone in church, with perhaps a little veiling not quite covering her face. The romance comes from the way she holds herself, the way she is dressed. And of course from the way the camera lingers on her!

Don't leave these figures, these women, these aspects of yourself hanging around in your head like lost souls. Incorporate them into your life.

Sunglasses are the twentieth-century equivalent of fans and veils. People use sunglasses to hide themselves. There is a particular art to taking off sunglasses, of choosing exactly the right moment to reveal yourself.

People work out their own ways of being mysterious. The outdoor California girl, for instance, has her own

1790s frock coat—dressing as the Scarlet Pimpernel himself and adapting the look to today with unusual costume jewelry.

special game of scrunching her hair up under a baseball cap, then pulling the peak down so that part of her face is hidden. Those California girls don't resemble old-fashioned ladies with fans and swirling dresses, but the effect is much the same.

Large floppy hats are mysterious too. The skill is simply to keep some part of your body, some part of yourself, hidden. A woman wrapped in a sarong is sexier than the woman wearing an itsy-bitsy-teeny-weeny bikini. Nobody knows whether the woman in the sarong has a bikini underneath or nothing at all. It starts the imagination working, makes people wonder, be intrigued, interested.

Anything to do with the past carries with it its own special air of enigma. You don't have to dress up in a Carmen costume and carry a fan. You can just take an old lace or silk handkerchief with you into the office instead of a box of Kleenex. Carry the past with you into the present.

The air of romance that should surround any woman, whatever her age, is not bought with expensive dresses. It is something that comes from deep inside. But small accessories, small touches of the past, can help bring out the female woman inside every woman. It is as if the old ring, old buttons, old fan picked up in a junk shop are the talismans that connect us to our ancestors.

Take off the dull mass-produced buttons from your dresses and suits, and instead sew on some lovely old pearly or beaded buttons or even some military ones.

Wear beautiful embroidered shawls from antique shops instead of cardigans.

Tie your hair up into an exotic turban.

A beautiful hat can transport a woman into another, simpler, age.

My favorite accessory—an old panama hat.

It's not a question of going back to the past but simply of taking what was good in the past and attaching it to the present. We are moving too fast into the future. Women should help provide stability, and enough sorcery to keep the past alive, and to prevent the shoddy elements of the present and the future from taking over.

Remind everyone of what is good in life, wear what is good, wear a fresh flower instead of a brooch, silk stockings on your legs, lace in your hair. Be close to nature, textures, the past, even while you are arranging multimillion-dollar deals—or perhaps especially then.

Women should certainly lose not an inch of the position they've gained over the years. But we must also make sure we don't lose ourselves.

A beautiful hat can at once transport a woman into another, simpler, age. In our house in England I have a room full of them. My favorite is an old Panama that's been chewed by a dog: it has holes in it and is bent in the wrong places. Admittedly there aren't many occasions I can wear this. Take a somewhat smarter version of a straw hat, something that fits and suits you, and stick flowers on it, fresh ones, silk ones, or a wreath of dried ones around the crown.

But an air of romance doesn't come only from wearing a marvelous old petticoat, or having your hair long; it comes from a certain individuality.

You don't need a great many clothes and colors in your wardrobe. When I was in *Our Mutual Friend* the art director decided there should be no color in any of the clothes. The only color should be in the skin, the faces, the individuality of the characters portrayed. The viewers were never aware of this technique, and even the critics didn't notice it. They just praised the series. It is your individuality, your fascination, that should be shown up by dress.

If you have beautiful green eyes, wear dark green satin. If reds help bring out the shape of your mouth and the tone of your skin, wear red, and try other bright colors. But having decided bright colors suit you, don't always wear bright colors. Remember that you change, your face alters, your personality is not always the same. Don't wear red if you're feeling moody and sexy, wear black instead. Let the clothes bring out your moods, the stages in your life.

If you're feeling predatory and vampish, why not try wearing some leather? Tina Turner wears short leather skirts; why shouldn't you, whatever your age?

If you're in a dreamy, feminine mood, wear one of the Laura Ashley creations.

Let your moods and looks control what you wear. Don't be dominated by the clothes, deciding to wear something simply because it is a beautiful dress. Too many women have walked into too many parties looking frightful because they liked a dress that didn't like them.

On the other hand, don't leave your best clothes unworn simply because they're your best clothes. Wear them, adapt them, make them a part of you, an extension of you.

If someone says, "What a beautiful dress," you hope they mean you look beautiful in that dress, not that the dress is terrific but you don't look that good.

If you're at a loss, wear white. White flatters most people. There's something so clean and fresh about white wool or linen, and its impracticality makes a statement, tells people you live your life with a certain flamboyance. White also brings out the color of your skin.

When you walk into a room, you don't want people saying, "Look at So-and-so—isn't her make-up good?" You want them simply to think how beautiful you are. It's the same with acting. If the audience is saying, "Oh, look, he's a terrific actor; look how well he's acting right now," he's lost it. If the audience is crying their eyes out because they were so moved and they believed you *were* that person . . . *that's* acting.

When I first arrived in Hollywood I was determined not simply to fit into a mold. I didn't have one pair of blue jeans. Not one. I wore peasant skirts made of Liberty cottons, which I had made myself with no pattern, just two widths of fabric at the top, four at the center, and six at the bottom. The skirts would flare out with no bulk at the waist. I love the feeling of cotton or natural fabrics next to my skin. They make me feel free, relaxed, myself.

A friend of mine has made a simple decision. She wears only two colors, black and white. She has decided they suit her, and, since she travels a great deal, it is important that she have adaptable clothes that mix and match well. Black doesn't have to be severe. She adds a brooch or a hat or a belt, and transforms a dress from office to evening in no time. The two-color decision gives her her own very individual look, with little inconvenience, perfect for travel.

My dresser when I was in *Amadeus* had much the same idea. She was a wonderful black lady who always wore black when she was working. Yet she could transform herself into a glamorous woman in no time. She

Costume jewelry can be great fun—and inexpensive!

My usual look in Hollywood when I first arrived—"peasant look" clothes.

always hid a hat, a pair of gloves, white beads, something that she could take out and add to the clothes she was wearing. She would be ready to go off to a premiere, to dinner, anywhere, in about five minutes flat.

Sally, my sister, has a talent for transformation, too. She works for an airline and carries clips for her shoes. When she goes out after work and isn't able to change, she can just put on a different pair of stockings and these little bows on her shoes, and she feels she has changed. She feels a new woman.

Much of the art of being romantic is feeling yourself to be romantic, desirable, feminine. If you don't feel terrific, you won't look terrific. You won't walk tall, you won't be sultry, you won't dare to flirt. Everyone knows the misery of going to parties or dinners and feeling dull and plain in clothes you didn't have time to change out of, or of wearing some marvelous dress that you are increasingly convinced is going to unzip or fall off or trip you.

Be yourself, that is the important point, and enjoy yourself. Be comfortable.

Sometimes be yourself by wearing no make-up at all. One of my greatest pleasures is not wearing make-up. I am always expected to be beautiful, to be on show. But my idea of heaven is not thinking about what I'm wearing, and not bothering with lipstick, eye shadow, anything.

Enjoy yourself with make-up, too. Give different looks to the same you: exotic one day, fresh-faced the next. I use make-up as paint, as part of the whole design. Paint your face, experiment, be anyone, any day, make your lips bigger, your eyes more sensual, bring out facets of your character in your changing, changeable face, the mirror of your soul.

I never plan what I'm going to wear, and what make-up will go with it—I rely on my instinct to take over at the time. If you go to work every day with the same make-up and same kind of clothes and you feel people don't notice you, wear something different, or wear your hair in a new way, or put on bright red lipstick, so that your colleagues are aware of you as a person, a woman, instead of a compact work machine.

One of my tricks, which I learned from a make-up artist, is to take a pillbox and chop pieces of lipstick off to make the pillbox into a palette, with all the colors you like. When you travel you don't have to take lots of lipsticks to change color all the time. If you're at the office wearing a light color, you can simply take out your lipbrush and your palette and change it to red. Also, you can mix colors. There is no make-up artist who doesn't mix colors.

To me, perfume is as important as dress or make-up in creating a romantic presence. It isn't that it should be noticeable. It shouldn't. You should choose a perfume that gives a man a sense memory of you, of the whole you; you as a personality, you as a person, you as someone bewitching.

Make your environment fragrant, have beautiful flowers around, spray fragrance in the bath and on light bulbs so that the heat makes the room full of the soft perfume.

The right fragrance can transform someone's attitude toward you. Too much of it, and he'll want to sit on the other side of the room. I promote Le Jardin, which has a light fragrance. I promote it because I like

Another Max Factor Le Jardin ad—inspired by the Fragonard painting,
wearing my wedding dress again, this time with a blue sash.

it, because a floral smell suits me well and I love flowers. When I first arrived in Hollywood I used to wear a fresh gardenia every day.

Remember that a smell can conjure up memories and desires: the smell of pastry recalls moments of childhood for me, sitting in the kitchen with my mother baking. A pine-wood smell can suddenly transport you back to other pine woods, in other times and places, to early childhood and beyond. The sense of smell has the strongest memory of all the senses. Make memory work for you.

Don't follow fashions: create your own fashions. Princess Diana has done this brilliantly, creating her own fantasy style within a strict lifestyle. But don't follow her way of dressing; make up your own.

Try wearing shiny thirties dresses or twenties flapper beads or the padded shoulders of the forties or the Laura Ashley romantic English look with plaids, petticoats, and bloomers.

But remember, a romantic presence doesn't come from having just pretty eyes and pretty clothes. A romantic presence comes out of subtlety, the way you project yourself, the way you use those pretty eyes. Invariably, it's noticing other people that transforms a well-dressed woman into a beautiful woman. If you look and don't see, it's a waste of time to have even the most lavish clothes, the most luscious, well-made-up eyes. It's what you see and how you reflect what you see that is the language and the communication.

Use your imagination—make drama out of your appearance.

My most successful transformation was, perhaps, during my visit to the producer of the Bond film all

Jenni, Katie, and I wearing our romantic Laura Ashley outfits.

those years ago.

In the ballet world if you're not five or ten minutes ahead of schedule, they won't let you attend the class. Therefore I was early. And to this day I am grateful I was early. Those minutes of waiting gave me a chance to perfect something that, I now believe, started my whole career.

Because I was early I went into the Grosvenor House Hotel next door to make sure my make-up and hair were okay. I was wearing a new coat, a suede coat with a raccoon collar, the first item of clothing I had ever really splurged on. Michael and his mother and I had agonized for a couple of days over whether I should also buy the expensive fur hat that matched the collar.

My mother, exuberant and extravagant as she is, decided I simply must have that hat: "Buy the hat. It makes the outfit."

"But I really don't have the money."

"Trust me," she said, "one day it will be worth it."

I bought the hat.

Wearing the hat I sat in the reception room, waiting for Harry Saltzman to see me, for what seemed like hours.

When I was finally ushered into the room, he ordered, "Take off your hat. Take off your coat."

I took off my hat, quite nervously, and my hair all came tumbling down over my shoulders.

He was entranced, amazed, delighted.

I had been practicing this maneuver in the Grosvenor House Hotel in the ladies' room, and the cloakroom attendant there watched me do this. I'm sure she must be chuckling to this day about how she saw me putting my hair up and taking my hat off. I was trying,

I suppose, to show him what I looked like without hair, with a "clean" face, and with long hair. And I didn't want to put my hair up in his office and then take it down.

As it turned out, my romantic gesture secured me the part. That maneuver alone is something anyone with long hair should occasionally delight men with. There is nothing more ravishing than a stern creature with hair up in a bun becoming, in just a moment, someone sensual and indulgently feminine.

Don't be too liberated, too severe on yourself, to allow yourself the occasional apparently artless female trick. What is wrong with flirtatious actions? Personally, I love men to open doors, to take off my coat for me. I like them to play their role and for them to allow me my femininity.

How boring life will be if women continue to be severe on themselves, to stride up and down corridors like men, never to stoop to such tricks as my hair trick. Where is the fun? Where is the excitement? The danger, the humor?

You don't want an average, sensible, down-to-earth life any more than I do. You want something remarkable, vivacious, occasionally wicked. You want sometimes to be a temptress, a superior lady with her hair piled up, sometimes a hard-working woman of the world.

Whenever I'm in a movie now, if there is a scene where my character has to submit to the man, the producer says, "Oh, it would be wonderful if you had your hair up, took one pin out, and let it tumble down." They all come up to me as if this were a completely unique idea.

I try not to smile.

After Harry had met me, he took me to his partner Cubby Broccoli across the street, and the two of them had an argument about who had discovered me first. Since the episode of "The Onedine Line," a BBC series in which they'd both seen me, had naturally reached them simultaneously, I could only reply that they both discovered me at once.

My successful transformation had won me the part of Bond's leading lady, and launched me on my career as a film star.

Don't be afraid. Use a little flair, a little imagination. Be the dramatic figure of your dreams. Discover yourself—live adventurously. Rent a fur coat for an evening, borrow a mink. If you've always wanted to make a grand entrance, hire the most lavish dress, the most lavish jewels, a fur coat, and make that entrance. You don't have to be rich, you don't have to be a film star, to look like a film star. Everything is within your reach, given a little ingenuity and some daring.

Don't be afraid. You can do it. That is one of the points about romantic living. Don't think people are going to laugh at you. You can carry anything off, and the first time you do carry off the fur coat, or the jewels, or the vast hooped ball gown, you'll feel very, very pleased. The right dress can bring out the actress in you.

11

Romantic Settings

O U R house in England could hardly be more romantic: wood-paneled library, croquet lawn, a sense of history, and peace. It lies in a valley near Bath, in Somerset, dreaming of the past.

Find your own romantic dream house and turn it into a sanctuary for your children and family.

An English friend of mine fell in love with a beautiful Long Island beach house. She couldn't afford it. Indeed, she could hardly have afforded one room of the place.

Instead of hankering after the American house she couldn't afford, she searched maps, the newspapers, real estate agents, advertisements for somewhere by the sea, imagining at best she'd find a seaside terraced

St. Catherine's—the perfect setting for romantic fantasy.

St. Catherine's.

house, but hoping for more.

Her determination paid off: just a short distance from London, in Essex, she came across a tiny, secret colony of beach houses in a spectacularly beautiful bird sanctuary.

None was for sale.

But she talked to a man walking along the beach and discovered that someone was thinking of selling theirs. It had just two bedrooms but a huge terrace overlooking the sea.

She bought the house. It's much smaller than the Long Island one, but it cost her well under $20,000 as opposed to over $500,000. And it is on the beach, a secret private beach, which only the birds and she and the other owners of the fifteen or so beach houses know about.

And what she had so loved about the Long Island house she had at her small Essex house: the solitude, the sea, the closeness to the elements, the beach, and the sense of open space. What makes her place exclusive is not the price but the bird sanctuary that prevents other people from using it.

There is always a way round any problem. A dream can come true. Dreams do come true. Again, and again, and again.

Find your own romantic setting.

My friend now huddles by the open fire in her beach house and watches storms in winter, goes running over the empty beach with her small daughter in summer, watches the sun rise and set. You don't need to be rich to find perfection.

St. Catherine's is our ideal romantic setting; the beach house is hers. Discover your own. Search for it.

LEFT: *Katie and Benson (our dog).*

BELOW: *The nursery at St. Catherine's.*

It's there—somewhere. To find it requires thought, imagination, determination.

Like our friend, we wanted to bring up our children close to the natural world. This is important for all children. They are more comfortable among birds and dogs and flowers and trees, the old timeless world, than among the office blocks and cars of our modern civilization. St. Catherine's Court has dogs and horses and cows and natural beauty. It is a very beautiful place for a child to grow up. What is more, there is room for all our family there. Among the many things we have lost this century is a sense of family. I want to be able to share my life with my parents, at Christmas, in the summer, eating together, having parties together, exploring the countryside together. A house should be somewhere you can share with those you love.

The atmosphere of a place is its most important ingredient, and the atmosphere of St. Catherine's is that of happiness and the family. You have to work at an atmosphere. It's the atmosphere that makes a setting romantic. The writer Jan Morris actually leaves beautiful music playing in her Welsh house when it is empty, because she feels it affects the mood of her house, makes it welcoming, as though the walls soak up the music. Similarly, happiness gives more atmosphere to a home than all the fine furniture and paintings in the world.

Make sure your friends and family come to your home, make it somewhere warm and welcoming for you and for them. In the midst of all the rush and bother of this century, your home should be your sanctuary, somewhere to be at peace, somewhere you can feel sane again, can talk easily to your friends, can contact your family.

St. Catherine's Court is somewhere we can re-create an old-fashioned world based on romance and the family. We don't play at being lords and ladies of the manor, but we do escape into a better, older world, close to the children, to nature, to our family. It is something we all need to do if we're going to cope with the demands of our fast modern life. Here, all over the soft stone, grow ivy and flowers. I love the animals and crests on the crumbly walls and the way the leaves of the mulberry tree press against the window of the drawing room. Everywhere, it seems, there are leaves pressing against the leaded windows: the leaves of yew trees, fir trees. The windows throw squares of sunlight on the wooden floors, and we keep fresh flowers on the white window sills.

There were no gardens here when we first came, only weeds. But it was still ravishing. We could imagine what it had been like, what it could be like. We discovered steps that had been buried for years in weeds and brambles. There were no fences. We had to cut away through masses and masses of nettles. We cut away and cut away and discovered two fish ponds with natural flowing water. The previous owner didn't know they existed. They were completely overgrown.

The whole place was falling apart. The top floor, which is now the nursery floor, hadn't been touched for decades. It was a warren of small rooms, where the servants used to live.

For us, renovating St. Catherine's was paying a debt to the past, and expressing a hope for the future. I think that creating a home, in particular renovat-

The conservatory at St. Catherine's—a most romantic setting enhanced by exotic flowers.

Old books lend so much atmosphere…the library at St. Catherine's. We collect old books from all over, especially books on the history of the house.

ing an old house, is always a positive act. You are creating your own world, with respect for the past. If you do it well, it is a great achievement, and one that provides great comfort. In this modern age we are too often cut off from the past. Oddly enough, one reason we were sold the house was because the owner was a red-headed Catharine. And when she saw another red-headed Catherine—little Katie—she felt that it was right, and we had it. Those kinds of connections are important, because connections—a sense of the past and the future—are necessary to the romantic life. None of us lives alone; we live with others, within time. A romantic setting is nothing without atmosphere.

Always find out about the place where you live: discover its history, its legends. Even if you live in a modern house, the land upon which it was built was there in the nineteenth century, in the eighteenth. Make it your business to know its history, to care for its past. Remember you too are a part of history. St. Catherine's has a long and rich history. It was given by Henry VIII to his beloved illegitimate daughter, but before that it was owned by Benedictine monks. There has been a church here since then called Katerina or St. Catherine's. Parts of the kitchen date back to 950.

We try to bring the past into the present: sitting up above the main doorway is a stone effigy of Bungie, the Elizabethan owner's faithful dog. We have named our golden retriever after him. Of course, the house needs a great deal of upkeep, and it would be hard to run without the money from my films and my husband's business. But your dream house, close to nature, close to the seasons, doesn't have to be expensive or big or costly to run.

Either look for the house of your dreams or turn wherever you are into a romantic setting.

I try to make wherever I am romantic. In my job I sometimes have to move from one dreary hotel room to another. It's essential not to give up, not just to accept that it's dreary. Never be downcast by your environment. If you don't like it, change it. The whole atmosphere of a room can be changed with just a few inexpensive touches.

Switch off electric lights, which show up the orange walls and avocado bedspreads of the hotel room, and replace them with flickering candlelight and the lush smell of scented candles instead of the smell of vacuum cleaners and detergents.

Buy fresh flowers, add your own lacy pillow to the bed, have some of your favorite books lying around, and bring your loved ones with you by having tiny picture frames to put by your bed.

Turn on some music, or bring your own favorite music, and in about twenty minutes that dull hotel room will be your own individual room.

Don't put up with living in gloomy places. Anywhere can be beautiful. It simply needs a little thought and imagination.

You are unusual, you are unique. Be true to your own tastes, however outlandish or odd they might seem to others, and you will create something as unique as you are. Frame your grandmother's patchwork quilt, cover a wall with hats, spend all your money on one beautiful painting.

At home as well as when you're traveling, you must be yourself. You mustn't accept someone else's vision of who you are or what is right or wrong. A strong sense of self is the secret behind excellence in every field—whether it's giving a good, unusual dinner party or decorating a room in your personal style. You must project your own fantasy of yourself. Not what you think someone else wants you to be. Sit in your living room and say: "Is this *my* room or is this the neighbor's room? Is this the room I've built for other people or is this the room I've built for *me*?" Only by developing your own vision will you furnish and decorate a room with flair.

Think about lighting first of all. A beautiful room can be spoiled by poor lighting. Place candles in the fireplace, lights behind plants, hurricane lamps on the floor. Use lighting that flatters, beguiles, makes mystery and beauty, but that can also be altered to provide good lighting for reading and writing.

In the tiny apartment where I stayed when I first came to Hollywood I *lived* on the floor because I couldn't afford a sofa. That was fine. I lived Japanese style, with cushions on the floor, picnics on the floor, a low coffee table, plenty of simple flower displays and plain colors. My luxuries were the occasional old plate or piece of cut glass bought at sale to add color and variety. I love deliberately mismatched old plates used together; they have an air of drama and the past that a perfect dinner service can never achieve.

When I could finally afford to buy a sofa, I still lived on the floor!

The New York loft where I stayed while acting in *Amadeus* was very stark—so I filled it with flowers. Fresh flowers every day.

Give your room, apartment, or house a particular

Our living room in Los Angeles—capturing the indoor/outdoor way of living.

Flower arranging at St. Catherine's.

atmosphere. Instead of buying a boring chair, think about putting in a small stained-glass window or buying French lace curtains or a big picture that transforms the room. Wherever you live, whatever your finances, don't play it safe. Go for the exotic, the marvelous, the outrageous, the beautiful. Don't make do with looking average. Spend that bit of extra time and trouble. Hang your collection of straw hats in your hall instead of smart wallpaper, have a cluster of old vases all on one table, pick wild flowers, buy or make embroidered cushions, fix kimonos to the walls instead of paintings.

It is easy, once you become used to your home, no longer to notice it. But it should be somewhere that interests you and pleases you every second you spend there.

Nothing need be expensive. In our house, St. Catherine's, we have a superb romantic bed, with pink and gray drapings hanging from the ceiling. It is not difficult to hang material from the ceiling to make a draped fabric canopy that falls around the bed, giving it the effect of a fourposter.

At the other end of the room is a small sitting area, and I recommend this idea to anyone who has the space: it is an excellent way for husband and wife to have their own private escape area for reading and being together. In our Los Angeles house, we have the same idea, only it's a separate room off the bedroom.

The bedroom should be the best room in the house, somewhere you want to spend time, for loving and living. The problem is that his ideas and yours about what is a romantic bedroom are likely to be quite different. Women usually favor floral, flouncy rooms,

Our bedroom, with its own sitting room area, at St. Catherine's.

whereas men like plainer, harder colors. Make sure you choose something that suits you both. A bedroom is where you should both feel comfortable, sexy, and happy.

David and I seldom disagree about decorations. Although he hasn't been trained as an architect, he is a brilliant designer and has a real feeling for how houses work. He actually designed the house in Los Angeles himself. But the bedrooms were one area where I feared trouble. He compromised with a gray-and-white bedroom in Los Angeles, which is a much cooler, more modern house, and a pink-and-gray one in St. Catherine's, which is lusher and nothing if not romantic.

Both bedrooms have fireplaces. Even when a fire's not alight, a fireplace provides a sense of warmth, and a focus for the room. In Los Angeles, every two or three weeks, I buy three stems of whatever tropical flower I can find that looks good; anything from Bird of Paradise, which are cheap and cheerful and in California grow in your backyard, to lilies. I place the three stalks and a bunch of greenery in the one big vase we have at the center of the mantelpiece.

In St. Catherine's we have a breath-taking view of the valley—a more traditionally English scene could hardly be imagined—and in Los Angeles we look out on our swimming pool and the main courtyard of the house. We have see-through curtains, so no one from the outside can see in but we can see out. Because we like to wake up very early, around five, we don't need curtains. We wake up with the sun and go to sleep when the sun goes down.

A good idea for transforming any bedroom into an

exotic place is simply to extend long curtains all the way around the room so that when you go to bed you draw the curtains and the room changes from a daytime area to a romantic, draped room. Use velvet curtains, oriental cottons, or any material you like.

Have old unmatched linen pillowcases—linen that has been washed and washed until it feels like silk. You can buy freshly laundered antique linens in flea markets. Fresh fabrics, real cotton, feel good against the skin, and a romantic bed should be sensual, luxurious, beautiful.

Bathrooms are nearly as important as bedrooms for the romantic. They shouldn't be just functional rooms. They should be places to bathe together, talk together, relax together. In a bath you can just soak away all the worries and troubles, and feel them pour away with the water down the drain. Plenty of bath essence, hot water, a bottle of champagne or chilled wine (we have an especially wide sill around all our tubs for this very purpose), the right music, the right man. It's my idea of heaven. Let him give you a facial massage as you bathe, or you give him one. The way to become an expert masseuse is simply to think what feels good to you, and then do that to him. Massage the forehead, the neck, the head, let him feel all those anxieties being smoothed away.

Put together a tape of your favorite music—Vivaldi, *La Bohème*, the Beatles, whatever it might be—so you don't have to keep getting up to change the music.

In our Los Angeles bathroom we have a sunken Jacuzzi bathtub with a mirrored wall and plenty of plants inside and out, climbing against the window from our jungle garden. The mirror exaggerates the

Old fashioned bath time—my bathroom in St. Catherine's, using existing tub and basin and hiding the uneven ceilings with romantic tenting.

Romantic bath time in Los Angeles. Candles lend a special glow.

quantity of plants, makes the room feel as though it is a mass of greenery.

Use tricks, use your imagination, and keep altering your environment as you alter and develop.

12

Romantic Meals

My youngest sister, Anne, was on her first date with her future husband at a New York restaurant. She accidentally tipped her chicken marengo into her lap.

She had to think of a way to save the situation. It wasn't exactly romantic to be sitting with a mass of food on her lap. She said, challenging him:

"If you were a real gentleman you'd change clothes with me."

"Okay," he said.

In the middle of the restaurant he took off his trousers and she took off her skirt and they exchanged clothes.

It was at this moment that they knew each was as crazy as the other. They knew they were meant for each other. They fell in love.

They walked back to his flat, holding hands, he in the skirt, she looking quite glamorous in his baggy trousers.

Food-in-the-lap isn't a technique I'd recommend. It could go seriously wrong. But her response does show a certain style.

Style is what counts. Your own style.

Donald and Anne are two of a kind, both madcap, adventurous, funny. They live their lives as they please, and they adore each other.

Personally, I favor more traditionally romantic meals by candlelight or by water, with roses on the table, although there is much to be said for informality. In *Somewhere in Time* the hero, played by Christopher Reeve, and the heroine, me, have a picnic on the floor of the hotel room after they make love. It is something I often do in real life. I like to turn the formality of a hotel room into something informal and adventurous.

When I first came to Los Angeles I used to get into the car, drive to the beach, park, walk around in the sun, then sit looking out at the sea with a picnic.

I didn't have to have anyone with me—I'd often go alone.

Sometimes another actress, Jenny Agutter, would go with me. We would buy an inexpensive sparkling wine and a little pot of cheap lumpfish caviar, some Wheat Thins and sour cream, and we'd take it all out to the beach and have champagne and caviar by the surf and toast the fact that we weren't sitting in an unemployment bureau in England. Those meals were more exquisite than the very best meals at the very best restaurants.

We were enjoying life for what it was and not wasting time feeling miserable about what it wasn't. Sometimes I think people overemphasize food. It's people and places and a sense of peace that turn a pleasant meal into a memorable experience. On our honeymoon in Italy, my husband and I stopped at a roadside café where the woman in the back room prepared us a pasta more delicious than anything all the fine chefs of France had prepared for us. We still eat pasta arrabiata at home. Good food doesn't require expense, or even a great deal of effort, just a little thought and an imaginative choice of setting.

Surprise your friends by producing a picnic at an outdoor concert, on the beach, on a walk. Where you eat is often as important as what you eat. Everyone I have spoken to on the subject of romance has referred to water. Somehow, when nothing makes sense anymore, looking at water, in particular eating beside water, can be calming. It gives a sense of peace and continuity. It connects us to the past and to the future, whereas so much else in our lives is disconnecting: the distance between people, the ring of the telephone, which interrupts your thoughts, the constant barrage of trivia from television and newspapers.

Once, when I lived in England with my second husband, Geep, we rented a London double-decker bus with a group of friends and drove off to Runnymede, where the Magna Charta was signed. Looking over the river Thames, we had champagne and beer and plenty of marvelous food. Usually double-decker buses are very restricting. It was a treat to have one all to ourselves, to be able to drink on it, eat on it, transform what was usually dull into a moving entertainment machine. Eat in unusual places—on buses, on rivers, on mountaintops. A romantic life is a varied life that creates magic everywhere, that turns a meal in a roadside café into an adventure, a picnic into heaven. Romantics are restless, always trying new things, new places, looking for heaven on earth and sometimes finding it in the most mundane places. Drive off to Cornwall and buy fresh lobsters, rent a thatched cottage by the sea and buy fish from the fishermen. Don't stay in your hometown eating the same food in the same ways; take off to other places, not necessarily glamorous places, but places where you can discover a perfect restaurant, a gorgeous wine bar, a cozy diner with homey food. Don't be trapped.

When I first arrived in California I couldn't believe how warm it was, and every morning I would breakfast in my little back garden with freshly squeezed orange juice and some fresh fruit. Sometimes, because I had very little money, I would just buy a bit of fruit, perhaps a few perfect strawberries. But I would turn those strawberries into a feast. I would make sure to savor each one—its texture, its color, its taste.

I still like to have breakfast outside, in a garden, on a balcony. Make sure you breakfast outside sometimes, even if it's only when you're on holiday.

Breakfast needn't be anything very complicated. David's favorite breakfast is a sort of scrambled egg with a little garlic in the butter. You add grated cheese and sesame seeds and put it under a very hot grill, or broiler, while it is still pretty wet on top. It puffs up like a soufflé. It looks sensational, and you can cut it up and add sour cream and chili sauce. It can stay in the frying pan all the time you're doing this.

A warm morning, with freshly squeezed orange juice, my scrambled egg soufflé, and the scent of orange blossoms in the air as we sit outside—that's our idea of bliss.

Of course, breakfast in bed is another treat that should be indulged in whenever possible. But don't cook anything messy and complicated.

Dinner by candlelight is another essential for the romantic life, because it flatters and it transforms. It transforms an ordinary room to somewhere mysterious, timeless, and while the two of you talk it seems you are two new people as your eyes watch each other through the soft firelight. In St. Catherine's we have a long, long table where we dine by the light of candles and sometimes with a roaring fire.

Always have candles handy. Candles shouldn't be only for celebrations. They can make every day into a celebration, make tired, hard-worked faces look less tired, and bring a little of the eternal into the everyday.

For the same reason, try to have a real fire sometimes, and cook when you can over an open fire. Men enjoy cooking over a fire. Watching a fire burn can take you out of the here and now, out of your busy life and make you peaceful.

My ideal romantic dinner is, of course, for two: with candles, an open fire, good wine, David, and a simple meal of fish and sorbet, something light and full of taste that doesn't weigh heavily on the stomach.

When you cook for a group of people—either a barbecue or a formal dinner—don't try to show off. If you're an excellent cook, cook something magnificent. If you're not, don't try to prepare a difficult meal that will make you bad-tempered and exasperated. And

ABOVE: *My sisters, Sally and Anne, and I pose with baby Katie after a family meal.*

LEFT: *Elizabethan dining room at St. Catherine's. The mood is always special with candlelight.*

don't worry too much about how you look, how you appear. Your concern should be with your guests, not yourself. You're not the star of the occasion, you're the director of all the stars, your guests.

Whether a meal is for one or for twelve the rules are the same: organize it as if you were directing a show; cast it right, set it right, light it right. The famous host and director Alfred Hitchcock said, "For truly great conversation, there should never be more than six to dinner . . . if more, the conversation tends to dissipate, ideas begin to founder." Personally I'd put the maximum at twelve, ideally around a big round table.

Don't cast the show with all couples, or all single people, all extroverts or all introverts: try to achieve a good mix. And don't worry if things go wrong with the food. The friends have come to see you and the other guests, not to eat. Some people even argue that really superb food stops the flow of conversation because people are concentrating on the food, and muttering compliments about the food, rather than enjoying each other's company. I find this a comforting thought when disaster strikes one of my dinner parties.

If dinner is flagging, move people to different places. Don't be too rigid about this: if you have decided to move people after the second course, don't move them if the conversation is going marvelously. Firelight, candlelight, flowers will help to relax people. But as the hostess you must help too. You must ask the right questions to encourage conversation, to show people at their best.

Whether a dinner is intimate or a larger, more formal party, think a little about the setting. As I said, the setting, atmosphere, and other people matter more

Romantic outdoor picnic for two.

*An original and romantic centerpiece by Corinna Liddell using flowers,
quail eggs, and a variety of colored pastas.*

than the food. If all else is well, people will hardly notice the food. For instance, put some thought into a romantic flower display. Certainly don't have such a large bowl of flowers on the table that no one can see the person opposite. The more delicate the display, the better. Pick wild flowers, flowers from the garden, or a few leaves with roses. Or buy a large bowl and float some flowers in the water, in the Japanese manner. The Japanese have the right idea—less is more. Always make sure you are sensitive to the season, and change your flowers accordingly. Bring the outside world into your dining room—candles, flowers, music.

Picnic in a park, by a stream, anywhere—but make sure your hamper doesn't include anything too difficult to serve. Make mousses, bring marvelous cheeses and breads and plenty of good wine and fruit.

Prepare well but make it look impromptu. That is one of the secrets of great romantic occasions.

Cook together sometimes but make sure that one of you isn't landed with the job of scullery maid—peeling potatoes, washing carrots. If cooking is going to be fun, all the nasty chores have to be done first.

Just happen to have all the ingredients for a soufflé or sandwiches or sorbet, ready to hand, and preparing a meal can be a romantic event.

David is an expert at making chocolate soufflé. And I'm afraid his offer to girls to "come back and make chocolate soufflé" in his bachelor days proved tempting to many.

When auditioning for *Raiders of the Lost Ark* Steven Spielberg took the cooking game a little far, and turned it into something that could well have been a torture for those who don't like to cook. Instead of auditioning

The Orient Express trip to Venice. Seven months pregnant with Sean, wearing my belt as a "'20s" headband!

Our Fourth of July cake—St. Catherine's, 1985.

actresses in the normal way, with a screen test and lines to say, he talked to them in his kitchen while, at his insistence, they made baba au rhum. He thought the kitchen brought out a person's real self. I didn't get the part, but I thought I made a terrific baba au rhum.

So if you do cook with a friend, make sure your real self is one you wish to reveal to him right then.

Throw the occasional terrific party. For a birthday of David's I arranged a surprise party in a Mexican restaurant. It was a theme party—and the theme was hunting, shooting, fishing, polo. It was a great success. Think of a theme. People love an excuse to dress up, to become children again.

A great idea is to stick a famous person's name on the back of each guest. Each one has to try to guess who he or she is by asking the other guests questions. It helps to break the ice.

Our Fourth of July party at St. Catherine's is always entertaining. We proclaim St. Catherine's independence from the rest of England, and celebrate in style, with hamburgers and a cake iced like the American flag. We invite the whole valley, our friends from all over the world, all professions and ages, and it is always a surprise. The first year the army landed, falling from the sky by parachute, on our lawn, and a bear-skin-clad band entertained us there.

Last year—desperate for entertainment on the day itself—we discovered a one-man-band "busker" in the streets of Bath. He came to the party and performed brilliantly for us. We had a clay-pigeon shoot in aid of a charity for the premature-baby unit of the local hospital—and the local poacher won! Some musicians who had never met before played wonderfully on the lawn all day and night and were so successful we thought they would form a band. Everything happened at the last minute, but it was wonderful because we'd simply allowed ourselves to be open to anything.

13

Gifts of Love

A ROMANTIC element in gift-giving is in the art of presentation. I believe that how you give a gift can be as important as the gift itself. Even the simplest gift can touch someone deeply if it has been bought or made with love and care and presented with imagination.

One of the best presents to give anyone is a collection of photographs. At a wedding, for instance, take along a Polaroid camera and a multiple picture frame; at the end of the reception, as you leave, give them the frame full of photographs. That way they have an immediate memento of the day and don't have to wait for the official photographs. The same can be done at a child's birthday party: the parent and child will be delighted.

Saying thank you is very important. People send flowers and never know what they look like. When my children were born, we received so many flowers that we took photos of the new family in front of them all and sent them to the well-wishers.

People like to receive something that shows you have thought about them, that you care about them. Wherever you live, whatever you do, really we all only have each other. It matters to know that other people love you enough to take time and trouble over you. That is why anything engraved with a person's name or initials is touching. Buy a crystal vase or a silver spoon or something from a junk shop or flea market or a smart shop, whatever your finances permit, and have it engraved. Another favorite gift is a traveling photo-wallet that has been inscribed. The engraving doesn't have to be flashy: it should, ideally, be in a secret place—at the bottom of the vase, for instance—where only you and he or she knows the name is hidden. Or have a message engraved. Anything that personalizes a gift is romantic, in this impersonal age of mass-produced goods. It is inspiring to think that in years to come someone might pick up the vase or the silver dish and see the message from you to your friend, engraved, or even just read the name, and wonder.

If you can sew at all, embroider your friend's name or initials on a big toweling dressing gown or one of those lovely old linen pillowcases. If you prefer, embroider a little pattern, just something to personalize it, to show you care. When my father was very ill and having an operation, I was desperate because I was in Los Angeles instead of with him. The night of his operation I took out one of Katie's *broderie-anglaise* pil-

Sean at three days posing in front of the flowers he received. This was our thank-you picture for the lovely gifts.

Fellow romantic and great friend, Corinna Liddell, with her birthday gift to me—a floral cake.

lowcases and embroidered "We love you P" (we children call him that) and forget-me-nots. Underneath I embroidered pictures of my mother, me, Katie, David, Sally, and Anne. It was a way for me to be close to him during that terrible time, when we all thought he might die, although we never said it. When my mother had rung me up to tell me he was having the operation, I said, "I'm coming on the plane . . . I'll just grab my handbag." But then I realized that my passport was in the Chinese embassy, because Red China had invited me to visit. So that night I had to embroider instead. He had another operation five days later, when he had just come out of intensive care, but by that time I was there. Before the operation, Sally and Anne and my mother and I stood round his bed and held his hands, and there was something going through our hands and arms. We never said, "Good-bye; you were a wonderful father . . . ," we just said, "See you tomorrow." It was very moving. He had the will to live because there was so much to live for.

While he was recovering, he kept his arm on my embroidered pillowcase, which touched me. It helped to give him strength, he said.

A gift people will always treasure is a drawing or painting of themselves, or their house, or their children. If you cannot draw or paint yourself, find someone who can and commission them. It could even be a portrait of a child's favorite teddy. The child would keep such a picture year after year, and pass it on to his or her own children.

People are always grateful for memories. Even if someone is rich, they cannot have enough memories; no one can.

Daracie, my best friend, makes porcelain dolls from an original mold and dresses them in clothes that look like those of a particular person. She also searches in antique and junk shops for old dolls that look a little like a certain person, and then renovates and dresses them accordingly. She made one that looked just like Goldie Hawn as a gift for her. Because dolls usually look like children, however, this present is best for a young child, but it makes a beautiful, thoughtful heirloom for anyone.

When Goldie was dating two Frenchmen at the same time, we gave her candlesticks with frogs climbing up them. I like presents that are funny and appropriate, that show some thought and humor.

Another friend, Corinna Liddell, transforms old printers' trays into miniature illuminated libraries, filling the shelves with tiny replicas of personal memorabilia, treasured photographs, books, and favorite objects. The one for Barbra Streisand featured her Oscars, gold records, and sheet music. Corinna calls them her miniature "lifestyles."

My agent has all my scripts leather bound, which is a beautiful present. She also does this for Tom Selleck, another client. Why not borrow someone's favorite book and return it on a birthday beautifully bound in leather?

I had a long-standing joke with my father that "when my ship came in" I'd buy him a Rolls-Royce. Of course, no one ever thought it would happen. Every now and again he'd ask, just as a joke, "Is there a ship on the horizon? Have sails been sighted?" Then one Christmas I sent him a card with a ship on it and inside it I wrote, "The ship's come in." The car was delivered

One of Corinna's original "miniature lifestyles," a unique, personal gift to be treasured always.

Darcie's gift to our friend Goldie Hawn, an antique doll made to look like her.

by a chauffeur, and at first I pretended I'd just borrowed it. Then I gave him the keys.

He wouldn't let go of the keys.

And my mother would go out in the snow in her slippers and wipe the snow off the car.

It wasn't a new Rolls. It was a twelve-year-old white Rolls, but it was smashing, and still is.

I gave an antique kimono to Andy Taylor, of Duran Duran, and I love to buy antique dresses for Katie or dolls in national dress.

Books, with an affectionate inscription, are always valued, especially old books, chosen with care: an old edition of *Mrs. Beeton's Cookery* for a keen cook, an old book about the universe for someone interested in the stars, a beautifully illustrated edition of *Alice in Wonderland* or *The Wind in the Willows* for a child.

Another idea is a collection of his or her favorite music: there are few people who aren't moved and touched by the beauty of music. Music has brought me some of the highest moments in my life. I don't even hear the music. I don't hear notes. I'm not even aware that someone has turned on a tape machine or that a record is playing—I'm in another world. What better gift than to give music that takes people out of themselves, onto a better, more spiritual plane? To record a special collection for them shows thought and affection.

One of my favorite presents is a miniature citrus tree a friend gave me. Something that lives is a thoughtful gift. Flowers or trees will grow and flower year after year, reminding people of you, and of your affection for them.

That is giving a memory and a thing of beauty.

The element of surprise, the unexpected, is important too. They arrive home and there is a mass of their favorite flowers, or flowers in their favorite colors, or an apple tree, or an orange tree, perhaps with a label plus a message and a great big ribbon around the trunk.

I love presents that are given with a little drama. One Christmas, David claimed he couldn't find the instruction book for something I'd given him, and he feared it had been thrown away. Crossly I marched over to the trash bag and started searching through it. At the bottom was a fur coat.

He had turned the tables on me, yet again.

Leave clues as to where a present might be, or wrap a tiny gift inside a huge parcel. It's the element of surprise, adventure, that in gift giving, as in everything, makes something special. Once I gave David a halter, because I'd bought him a horse.

To give that extra element of surprise and pleasure, why give presents only on birthdays and at Christmas? I like to give presents when I feel like it. In those days leading up to Christmas, which are so intense for a child, we once wrapped up little presents and let Katie open one on each day. They were only small things— an eraser, a crayon, some soap—but she loved it.

There was a marvelous line in one of my films, *Obsessed with a Married Woman*. A man who is single says to a woman who is married: "I guess you're booked for Christmas, Bank Holidays, Thanksgiving; how about Arbor Day?" Make up a day. Why not?

One spring, while on a cruise with friends, we decided it was Christmas. There was none of the pressure of Christmas: having to get the turkey right, having to do this and that, having to buy presents and cards for everyone. Instead, we just had all the fun, and of course all the eccentricity of celebrating Christmas at that time of year, in the hot sun.

Each person on the cruise chose one present, each for approximately the same amount of money, fifteen dollars. Each woman bought a woman's present and each man a man's present. They were all well wrapped, and we drew straws to see who would receive which present.

I had never enjoyed a Christmas quite so much!

A tradition that I grew up with was St. Nicholas. In Holland, where my mother comes from, Christmas is a very religious festival. The exciting time for the children is the feast of St. Nicholas, which happens in the beginning of December. The children put out carrots and water and bread for the reindeer. My father used to dress up as St. Nicholas in something red. The window would suddenly open and a whole lot of candy would be thrown into the room, and the children would dash for it. We would exchange tiny presents with one another. Everything was signed "With love from St. Nicholas." So, say you had a sister who might like a lovely bar of soap. You would wrap up the soap and write a clever rhyme that was faintly teasing (perhaps suggesting she should wash more). You had to write a rhyme of about two lines, and the point was to come up with funny little things that teased the person concerned. St. Nicholas was more fun than Christmas, when we received bigger presents.

The most important day in the year for the true romantic is St. Valentine's day.

This book is a plea for the return of romance to the

Cuddling Katie and taking time out to read and play with dolls. I have collected red-haired dolls for her since she was born.

Christmas in July aboard the Khashoggi yacht The Khalidia.

world, and for me Valentine's Day is a symbol of romance. It has all the ingredients—mystery, secret love, declarations of love. Don't just buy a mass-produced card and send it off with your name signed in it. That is not the way. A Valentine's card should be chosen with care. Buy an old card from an antique shop perhaps, or make one with care yourself. And when you send it off, do not sign your name. Instead, write a few words or more, in rhyme, that don't reveal who you are but do give a clue. Remember that romance is mystery, and mystery is romance.

Nonmaterial gifts can mean as much as material gifts, and sometimes much more. Organize a theater party or dinner for friends, offer to watch their children, let friends use your house while you're away for a week, swap homes with foreign friends, make homemade jam, or prepare a meal for someone.

While I was making *Somewhere in Time,* I suggested that our friend John Barry arrange the music, and one day, as a present, he phoned me and had the whole symphony orchestra play the music from *Somewhere in Time.* That moved me a great deal.

Our friend Leyla Khashoggi was asked by her husband what she would like for her birthday, and she replied that she wanted to take all her best friends on a yacht for a week.

On the plane on the way there she took out an enormous envelope and read out her gift for him. "We're having a baby."

Conclusion

It's hard to convey feelings—especially to write about them for an unknown audience. While I've been writing this book, however, and trying to communicate many of those feelings and beliefs that I hold most important, many interesting things have happened.

My husband asks incessantly when I will finish the book, so that we can continue to live the romantic life that I've been taking time away from to write about! My friends have helped enormously. They've all read the book as I've gone along, and to my surprise they've loved it. They recognized that they could follow their dreams themselves, and in playing out some of their romantic fantasies have invited us to join in. Some of them have suddenly (their spouses tell me) taken to

"Walking Home"—our favorite photograph, taken by best friend Steven Bickel.

inviting their husbands or wives to business lunches, sending surprises at odd times, and buying crazy hideaway houses in obscure but romantic locales. "Kidnapping" is now prevalent among my friends, and they are all sharing their ideas and successful outings with David and me.

I have received great pleasure in writing this book, if for no other reason than that it has allowed me to share my greatest gifts in life: the people who brought me into this world and those who have loved me and live with me—the people I love.

I thank all of you, readers and friends, for sharing in this quest for the romantic lifestyle, and I hope you will develop your own romantic style to share with your generations to come.